D1232334

DATE DUE

Lee Moves North

Lee Moves North

Robert E. Lee
on the Offensive

Michael A. Palmer

John Wiley & Sons, Inc.

New York • Chichester • Weinheim • Brisbane • Singapore • Toronto

This text is printed on acid-free paper.

Library of Congress Cataloging-in-Publication Data

Palmer, Michael A.
    Lee moves north : Robert E. Lee on the offensive / Michael A. Palmer.
        p.   cm.
    Includes bibliographical references (p. 171) and index.
    ISBN 0-471-16401-1 (alk. paper)
    1. Lee, Robert E. (Robert Edward), 1807–1870—Military leadership.
2. Command of troops. 3. United States—History—Civil War,
1861–1865—Campaigns.   I. Title.
E467.1.L4P25   1998
973.7'3'092
[B]—DC21   97-18182

Printed in the United States of America

10 9 8 7 6 5 4 3 2 1

To Russell F. Weigley

Contents

Preface

ROBERT E. LEE REMAINS one of the most enigmatic and controversial figures of the American Civil War. Despite his wartime prominence, Lee never penned a memoir, and while his correspondence reveals much about his strength of character, it reveals far too little of the inner workings of his military mind. For it was within the confines of that mind that Lee developed his operational plans, schemes that were almost never set to paper. As a result, historians have had to divine Lee's wartime intentions by studying impressive but still incomplete collections of relevant correspondence, less than explicit official reports, memoirs clouded by a writer's age or bias, and the details of the events themselves.

Given the need to interpret the mind and method of a commander who fought on the losing side of a conflict that itself remains a divisive topic, we should not be surprised to discover that the written work concerning Lee varies widely in its quality, tone, and conclusions. To some, Lee was a saintly figure, one of the greatest generals of all time, a commander who ultimately was defeated only because of the overwhelming power of a government willing to spend millions of dollars and tens of thousands of lives to wear down his gallant, but hopelessly outnumbered, Army of Northern Virginia. At the other extreme are those who have argued that the historic Lee has too often become more myth than man, and that the "real" Lee was a soldier whose faults were so marked that he not only failed in his efforts to defend the Confederacy, but also was himself a cause of its eventual undoing.

Passing historic judgment on Robert E. Lee as a military commander is no easy task. Despite what Lee's supporters and detractors have often claimed, Lee's record as a general does not lend itself to simple, or obvious, conclusions. Commanders, after all, should be judged by the results they achieved in the field, and not on quotations, pithy or otherwise, drawn from their writings. Lee fought and won some of the most spectacularly successful campaigns and battles of the nineteenth century. In the late spring of 1862, during the Seven Days, he saved Richmond from imminent capture. In the campaign that followed in northern Virginia, Lee outmaneuvered, outfought, and nearly destroyed another Union army. At Chancellorsville in May 1863, Lee turned the tables on an attacking Federal force almost three times the size of his own army and threw it back across the Rappahannock River in defeat and humiliation. In the spring and summer of 1864, Lee waged a stubborn and inspired defense against a much larger and better equipped Federal force. Such accomplishments speak of genius. But what of Lee's failures: the abortive Maryland invasion of 1862, the disastrous Gettysburg campaign of 1863, and the lesser known Bristoe Station fiasco of the following fall? Any general responsible for three such marked failures could easily be considered guilty of incompetence.

My purpose in this book is not to render a historical judgment on Lee as a general. My intent is not to try to convince the reader that Lee was either a great, or a poor, commander. In my mind, the man who won the battle of Chancellorsville had to be an inspired leader and a commander of note, perhaps even a genius. Do historians not consider Napoléon a great captain, despite the fact that he did not win all of his battles, despite the fact that he, too, ultimately met defeat?

Of course, to state as fact Lee's genius does little to explicate his defeats, just as claiming that he was a blunderer fails to explain his many victories. That being the case, what I offer in this work is an explanation to a question that has always intrigued me: What was it in the nature of Lee's generalship that enabled him with 43,000 men to defeat an army of 110,000 at Chancellorsville, but two months later caused him to lose at Gettysburg, where his army of 70,000 was arrayed against, relatively speaking, a mere 95,000 Yankees? Did he and his lieutenants simply have a couple of bad days? Or were there other factors at work? If so, what were they?

In an effort to answer these questions, this work will focus on three of Lee's campaigns—Maryland (September 1862), Gettysburg (May–July 1863), and Bristoe Station (October–November 1863). Two elements link these three undertakings. Obviously, all were failures; in fact, they were the only unsuccessful campaigns Lee waged until the final, unwinnable, and utterly hopeless struggle of the spring of 1865. Second, all three were strategic offensives, and the only strategic offensives that Lee undertook as commander of the Army of Northern Virginia. Could the strategic offensive, then, be the shared thread, the common denominator that might help to explain Lee's failures? Or is the link purely coincidental?

The relationship between the strategic offensive and Lee's defeats was, in fact, one of causation. Lee's approach to command, one that enabled him to achieve marked successes whenever his army fought on the strategic defensive, failed him miserably when he adopted the strategic offensive. Why? This work will examine Lee's three unsuccessful strategic offensives in an effort to identify those elements of his generalship that can account for his failures. The traditional explanations proffered for his defeats—insufficient manpower and supplies—are inadequate, because Lee was always outnumbered and outsupplied but did not lose all of his battles. Nor can crossing the Potomac into Yankee territory be considered the ultimate problem, since the army never left Virginia during the Bristoe Station campaign and yet failed just as miserably, albeit on a smaller scale. The fact remains that between 1862 and 1864 Lee won whenever he fought on the defensive, as he did at Fredericksburg. He won when he switched from a defensive to a tactically offensive posture, as he did in the Seven Days and at Chancellorsville.[1] Lee won as well when he went over to the strategic counter-offensive, as he did to meet the drive south of the Federal Army of Virginia in the summer of 1862, a campaign that culminated in the battle of Second Manassas. But when Lee took the strategic offensive with his own army—that is, when Lee moved not to counter an ongoing Federal operation in northern Virginia, but to drive north himself—he failed in each of his three attempts.

What, exactly, were the factors that undermined Lee's army when he undertook his strategic offensives? Most of the themes I will address here—the differing strategic concepts embraced by Lee and President Jefferson Davis, Lee's penchant for the offensive, his dislike of the details of staff work, his decentralized approach to command and control, and his strategic parochialism, to name a few—have been discussed, and ably so, by other historians. Over the past century numerous commentators and historians have questioned Lee's near-apotheosis as a commander.[2] But those who have been critical of Lee have generally failed to draw a clear connection between his shortcomings, be they alleged or real, and his performance on the battlefield. Lee, after all, did not lose—but won—most of his battles. That being the case, my intention is to couple Lee's supposed shortcomings, especially his differences with President Jefferson Davis over grand strategy, to his operations in the field and to explain how the unique pressures of the strategic offensive magnified what were otherwise real, but less consequential, weaknesses.

Since my intention is not to contest the work of Lee's critics or supporters, but in many ways to explain why both are, in part at least, correct though at the same time incorrect in their assessments of his generalship, I have not allowed this work to become, either in the narrative or the notes, a historiographical discourse. While I have addressed, especially in the concluding chapter, historiographical questions concerning interpretations of Lee's generalship, I have chosen not to cite each and every major historians' take on the myriad and often minute issues concerning Lee's campaigns and battles addressed throughout this book. I offer my narrative as a work of synthesis, of new interpretation, based on the information presented and adequately cited, and not as a critical analysis of a vast and complex literature. My belief is that the professional historians who will read this volume already know, and do not need to be told by me, what Archer Jones, Tom Connelly, or whomever wrote about a given issue; whereas the nonprofessional reader, and there are many with an interest in the War between the States, quite frankly does not care.

1

The Maryland Campaign

"I Would Have Fought and Crushed Him"

AUGUST 31, 1862, dawned dreary and overcast. A light rain fell on the bloodstained fields near Manassas, Virginia, where the bodies of thousands of American soldiers—Yankees and Rebels alike—marked the lines of battle along which the opposing armies had toiled. In a classic engagement, Confederate States General Robert E. Lee had "handsomely whipped" Major General John Pope's Federal Army of Virginia and driven it from the field.[1]

The Second Manassas campaign was a masterpiece of maneuver and battle. In mid July, Lee, who had only just forced back Major General George B. McClellan's Army of the Potomac from the gates of Richmond, shifted his attention to Pope, then moving south toward Gordonsville. In a six-week-long campaign marked by hard marching and hard fighting, Lee outmaneuvered and outfought the boastful Pope—the western general who had come east to teach the boys how to whip the Rebels. When the Federals appeared to have stabilized their position along the Rappahannock River, Lee dispatched Major General Thomas Jonathan "Stonewall" Jackson on August 24 on a march around Pope's right flank. The daring maneuver

1

drew the Federals into battle. Throughout the day of August 29, Jackson's near-isolated wing[2] clung desperately to its position along Stony Ridge, just north of the Warrenton Turnpike near Bull Run. When the next day dawned clear and bright, Pope chose to discount reports of the arrival of Rebel reinforcements, ignored the threat to his flank, concentrated his forces against Jackson, and resumed the attack in the afternoon. But as the bluecoats pressed forward against Stonewall's line, Major General James Longstreet led the right wing of Lee's army against the Federals' left flank and drove them back in defeat and disarray.

Despite the obvious success of a remarkable campaign capped by a brilliant victory, the commander of the Army of Northern Virginia remained disappointed and frustrated. In Lee's opinion, Federal armies had four times during the past four months evaded total destruction. He believed that during the Peninsula campaign, General Joseph E. Johnston had twice missed opportunities to "crush" McClellan's Army of the Potomac—first during the fighting near Williamsburg and then later at Seven Pines.[3] Lee, after replacing Johnston in command, had himself failed to do more than drive McClellan back, admitting after Malvern Hill that "under ordinary circumstances, the Federal army should have been destroyed."[4] Lee envisioned his subsequent northern march against Pope as a move designed not simply to drive the beaten Federals into the fortifications that guarded Washington, D.C., but to engage and to destroy the enemy army in the field. Second Manassas, while a noteworthy victory, had not been the annihilatory triumph Lee had sought.[5] During the fighting on August 29 and 30, Pope lost over ten thousand men, but Lee's army suffered slightly more than nine thousand casualties itself. Lee knew that the Federal losses would be more quickly and easily replaced than those of his own army. Of more immediate concern were reports that the lead elements of McClellan's army, withdrawn by sea from the peninsula, were already in northern Virginia. In fact, some of McClellan's troops had fought with Pope at Manassas.

Nevertheless, on the morning of August 31 Lee held the initiative. But what was to be done? Reports from Major General J. E. B. Stuart's cavalry indicated that Pope had retired to a strong position near Centreville, about four miles beyond Bull Run.[6] Since the continued rain threatened to render the stream impassable, Lee suspected that a direct pursuit would be difficult and, at best, do little more than hasten Pope's retreat toward Washington.

Lee decided to conduct a personal reconnaissance, hoping to gain not only a better understanding of the situation on the other side of the hill, but also a sense of the mood and state of his own army. He donned his rubber poncho and overalls, called for Traveller, his gray mount, and, accompanied by Jackson, rode toward Bull Run.[7]

While the two generals had achieved a marked triumph, the campaign they had fought had been somewhat out of character for them both. Before the start of the Seven Days, many Confederate officers and soldiers viewed Lee as a defensively minded engineering officer, referred to derisively as "the King of Spades" because of his predilection to entrench, whereas Jackson had performed brilliantly when operating on his own in the Shenandoah Valley, but had proved hesitant when his command first joined the Army of Northern Virginia during the Seven Days. Nevertheless, during the march north against Pope, Lee's newfound aggressiveness combined with Jackson's ability to operate independently to force Pope's battered army back to the outskirts of the Federal capital. By August 1862 Lee and Jackson had become the driving force, and the brain trust, of the Army of Northern Virginia.

The senior member of this team was Robert Edward Lee, a Virginian and the fifth son of Henry "Light-Horse Harry" Lee, himself a general officer of note during the American Revolution.[8] The younger Lee graduated in 1829 from the United States Military Academy at West Point, New York, ranked second in his class. During the Mexican War he served on the staff of Winfield Scott during the expedition against Veracruz and

Mexico City. After the war, Lee returned to West Point as su-
perintendent, commanded the Second Cavalry Regiment, and
led the detachment of marines that seized John Brown during
his infamous fall raid of 1859 at Harpers Ferry, Virginia. When
the prospect of civil war became reality early in 1861, Scott,
then the senior officer of the U.S. Army, offered Lee the position of field commander, but the latter declined and accepted
instead the command of the military forces of the state of Virginia. Lee subsequently gained a general's commission in the
Confederate States Army and waged his first campaign in the
western and heavily pro-Union counties of his home state. Despite Lee's lackluster performance, President Jefferson Davis
chose Lee as military adviser and, when General Joseph E.
Johnston fell wounded at Seven Pines on May 31, 1862, named
Lee to take over the command of the army. There followed the
Seven Days' battles and the march against Pope that led to the
field of Second Manassas.

To most of his soldiers, Lee cut a manly and noble figure.
Arthur James Lyon Fremantle, a British officer and observer of
the Confederate war effort, noted that Lee was "the handsom-
est man of his age I ever saw . . . tall, broad-shouldered, very
well made, well set up—a thorough soldier in appearance; and
his manners are most courteous and full of dignity . . . the per-
fect gentleman in every respect."[9] But beneath the poncho and
the stoic exterior, Lee, though only fifty-five, was aging quickly,
his hair and beard graying and his heart growing weaker under
the strains of the war.

At his side that morning rode Stonewall Jackson, just short
of six feet tall, with piercing blue eyes that earned him the
moniker "Old Blue Light" from some of his men.[10] Born in
1824 in western Virginia, he was an 1846 graduate of West Point
and, like Lee, a veteran of the Mexican War. But Jackson chose
not to remain in the army. In 1851 he accepted a teaching post
at the Virginia Military Academy. He joined the Confederate
States Army after Virginia's secession and commanded the
forces in the Shenandoah Valley. There, during the spring 1862

campaign, Jackson demonstrated that he was as mercurial as Lee was stoic. The overtly and deeply religious Stonewall avoided Sunday battles, but drove his hard-marching men relentlessly. For those officers who questioned their commander's ideas, or sanity, Jackson was quick to order arrest and court-martial. To some of his soldiers he became the eccentric "Tom Fool Jackson," to others just "Old Jack."

The appearance of the two generals and their staffs attracted the long-range fire of some Federal batteries. Pope's army, while bloodied and driven back, was evidently not yet in full retreat. But as Lee and Jackson looked out over the rain-swollen stream and considered the natural strength of the Union position around Centreville, they became convinced that the situation called for maneuver, not direct pursuit.

Lee decided to try, once again, to outflank Pope's army. Since Jackson's command was on the left, Lee directed Stonewall to initiate yet another flanking movement. Jackson's divisions would cross Bull Run at Sudley Springs Ford and would follow a country road that led to the Little River Turnpike south of Arcola.[11] From there, Jackson's troops would march southeast along the pike toward Fairfax Court House, where the road crossed the Warrenton Turnpike—Pope's main line of retreat via Annandale and Alexandria to Washington.

Later that morning, Lee met with the commander of his right wing—Major General James Longstreet. "Old Pete," as he was known to his soldiers, was a forty-one-year-old South Carolinian.[12] Like Lee and Jackson, Longstreet was fairly tall (nearly five feet eleven), a graduate of West Point, and a veteran of the Mexican War. Longstreet, whose gallantry had earned him the brevet (temporary) rank of major, remained in the army after the war, serving mostly in the West. In the spring of 1861 he made the painful choice to "go South" when his home state seceded. He had fought with, and gained notice in, the Confederate army in the East since First Manassas and had performed well in the Peninsula campaign and under Lee's command during the Seven Days. At Second Manassas Longstreet's flank attack ensured Pope's defeat and retreat, although there were some in Lee's army who believed that Longstreet had delayed his advance unnecessarily, prevaricating during the afternoon of August 29 despite Lee's requests to attack.[13] In this instance, Longstreet's caution and judgment proved superior to Lee's, and when the attack commenced on the thirtieth, it struck the Federal left with tremendous force and swept all before it.

The following morning, as Lee explained his decision to march around Pope's flank, Longstreet listened attentively and nodded in agreement. He knew firsthand the strength of the position around Centreville, one which the Confederates themselves had fortified the previous winter.[14] Lee directed that Longstreet's divisions remain on the battlefield until the tail of Jackson's column cleared Sudley Springs Ford. Longstreet would then follow, to be replaced along Bull Run by the division of Major General Daniel Harvey Hill, whose troops were just arriving from Richmond. While the distasteful duty of burying the dead would fall to Longstreet's men, they would also have the opportunity to more fully harvest the booty rapidly retreating Yankee forces always left behind.[15]

While Lee, Jackson, and Longstreet all agreed on the chosen course of action, they must also have recognized that the planned flank march, while certainly worth undertaking against a commander of the caliber of John Pope, nonetheless offered no guarantee of success. Jackson's battle-weary troops were about to undertake a roundabout, twenty-mile flank march, a third of which would be conducted over a rain-soaked, secondary country road. Pope's army near Centreville was positioned astride the Warrenton Turnpike, less than seven miles from Fairfax Court House. For the march to succeed, John Pope had to remain blind to the threat to his rear and slow to retreat. While the former was a distinct possibility, the latter, given the beating the Army of Virginia had suffered, seemed unlikely.

Three factors suggest that Lee and his lieutenants considered an alternative plan, although no record exists of any such discussion. First, given the capabilities of three generals such as

Lee, Jackson, and Longstreet, it seems likely that they would have reviewed possible courses of action beyond the completion of the planned march. What if Pope did adequately cover his flank or, more likely, retreated before Jackson reached Fairfax Court House? Second, the memoirs of members of Jackson's and Longstreet's staffs suggests that they viewed the trek around Pope's right as little more than the preliminary march necessary to cover the ultimate movement of the army northwards—toward the Potomac River.[16] As G. Moxley Sorrel, who served on Longstreet's staff, wrote: "General Lee took his army forward to the Potomac. Only a detachment of the enemy was encountered by Jackson, and this was at Chantilly, where toward dark, and in a furious storm, there was a short combat in which Major-General Kearny was killed and left in our hands."[17] Third, the speed and equanimity with which Lee, Jackson, and Longstreet subsequently made the transition to a new and daring plan suggests that such an alternative course had been discussed beforehand. After all, if Jackson's left hook failed to find Pope's right flank, as might well be expected, Lee's army would be perfectly positioned to continue its march to the north and west and to cross the Potomac River into Maryland.

As Lee and Longstreet conferred near a high railroad embankment, the cry "Enemy cavalry" punctuated the air.[18] A detachment of soldiers guarding some Union prisoners suddenly scurried over the embankment, a movement that frightened Traveller and caused him to rear. Lee was fortunately dismounted, but the reins were tangled around his wrists. As the commanding general was thrown violently to the ground, he broke his fall with his hands, badly spraining both wrists and breaking the small bones of one hand.[19] Major Walter H. Taylor, one of Lee's staff officers, wrote: "[Lee] had no use of either hand, and for some days each arm had to be carried in a sling. He could not ride his horse, and for some time thereafter moved in an ambulance. This was sore trial to the general's patience."[20] It was, along with the sour weather, a bad omen for the start of a new campaign.

AS LEE NURSED HIS SWOLLEN WRISTS, about noon Jackson's troops began their movement toward Sudley Springs. Major General Ambrose Powell Hill's "Light Division" led the column. "The march was over a single-track country road," Longstreet wrote, "bad enough on the south side of the river, much worn through a post-oak forest over quicksand subsoil on the north side." [21] It was nearly dark before the tail of Jackson's column cleared the ford and Longstreet's men joined the march. "If Jackson wished to baffle," Longstreet later recalled, "his gun-carriages could not have made deeper cuts through the mud and quicksand."[22]

Nevertheless, by the end of the day Powell Hill's men had reached the Little River Turnpike and marched to the southeast as far as the Pleasant Valley Baptist Church, just west of the line between Loudon and Fairfax counties.[23] Despite the late start, the state of the roads, and the fatigue of the men, in eight hours Jackson had covered nearly eleven, and the worst, of the twenty miles to Fairfax Court House.

Ahead of Jackson's infantry, Jeb Stuart's indefatigable troopers were also on the turnpike, having pushed cross-country meeting minimal opposition. Stuart's probes revealed what he termed "one continuous roll of wagons going toward Fairfax Court House."[24] That night Stuart, with Brigadier General Beverly H. Robertson's and Fitzhugh Lee's brigades, camped on and around Ox Hill.

Despite the movement of wagons to the rear, Pope was not—at least not yet—in retreat.[25] Orders from Washington directed him to hold on at Centreville, even if it meant a renewal of the battle.

Nor was Pope completely oblivious to the dangers to his flank and rear.[26] The appearance of Stuart's men near Fairfax on the afternoon of the thirty-first alerted the Federals and prompted Pope to dispatch a brigade-size scratch force of infantry, cavalry, and artillery from the Third Corps to the crossroads.[27] Early the next morning, Pope, concerned about a possible threat to his flank, ordered Major General Edwin V.

Sumner to conduct a brigade-size reconnaissance north from Centreville "not less than 5 miles" toward the Little River Turnpike.[28] If the brigade found any sizable force of Confederate infantry, Pope directed Sumner to "withdraw." Then, in the late morning, reports reached Pope that indicated that a strong column of Rebel infantry was marching around his flank. Union Major General Fitz-John Porter wrote that he could see "the dust and flags" of the Confederate columns moving north."[29] At 11:00 A.M. Pope relayed the information by telegraph back to Washington.[30] But an hour passed before he initiated any countermoves: at noon Pope ordered Major General Irvin McDowell, commander of the Third Corps, to march to Germantown, just west of Fairfax Court House. "Jackson is reported advancing . . . with 20,000 men," Pope wrote. "Move quickly."[31] The Federal commander saw not just a threat, but also an opportunity. Pope planned not just to block Jackson, but also to sidestep the Army of Virginia to the right and to counterattack the next day along the Little River Turnpike.[32]

For Lee's soldiers, September 1, 1862, dawned clear, if not sunny.[33] Stuart broke camp and rode out "to connect" with Jackson, finally locating the head of the general's infantry columns near Chantilly. Stonewall's vaunted "foot cavalry" had resumed their march at dawn, but without their usual celerity. Despite the fact that the Little River Turnpike offered far better going than the country road, Hill's van division had covered less than three miles.

Stuart, accompanied by Major Heros von Borcke and Lieutenant Chiswell Dabney, found "Old Stonewall," as von Borcke later recalled, with "his outposts very much amused at the effect of the rifle practice of some of his marksmen upon a squad of Yankee cavalry."[34] Stuart reported the weakness of the Federal defenses between Chantilly and Fairfax Court House. "[N]o force but a small one of cavalry was discernible nearer than Centreville," he assured Stonewall.[35] The road into the Union rear appeared open.

And so it was. Late the previous evening an alarmed and well-informed McClellan, at his headquarters in Alexandria, had sent an urgent telegram to Major General Henry Wager Halleck, the Union general in chief, warning that "Pope's right is entirely exposed" and the critical road junction at Fairfax Court House unguarded. McClellan warned: "I have no confidence in the dispositions made as I gather them—to speak frankly, & the occasion requires it, there appears to be total absence of brains & I fear the total destruction of the Army."[36]

But Jackson, according to Stuart, was in no hurry and chose not to press the advance but to wait for Longstreet to come up.[37] By then, of course, the day would be late and whatever opportunity, if any, that existed to break into the rear of Pope's army would be lost. It was noon before Stuart received his orders. Robertson's brigade would deploy to the south of the turnpike to guard Jackson's right against any Federal move north from Centreville. Stuart, despite the fact that Jackson ordered him "to proceed cautiously" along the turnpike, advanced with Fitz Lee's troopers in an effort to "force" a way through to Fairfax Court House.[38]

Stuart's men, moving forward as skirmishers, reached a position less than three miles northwest of the courthouse where, according to their commander, they fell "into an ambuscade" and discovered the "wooded ridges" on either side of the road firmly held by Federal infantry and artillery.[39] "It was plainly indicated," Stuart concluded, "that the enemy would here make a stand." If the Federals were to be driven back, Jackson's men would have to do the driving. Stonewall ordered Stuart to take Lee's brigade and move north around the Federal right, while Powell Hill's division formed into line of battle.

Stonewall's troops had set no marching records that day. As one Alabama soldier recalled:

> Our march was slow, with frequent stops, lasting sometimes as long as an hour, as if to give time to our generals to locate the true positions of the enemy. We moved on in this way un-

til we had fairly turned Pope's position at Centreville, and was just about to get in his rear when he took the alarm and began to move his troops to prevent it.[40]

Not until 4:00 P.M. on an afternoon grown so dark that some reported it as evening, had Hill's lead brigades finally come into contact with the Federals.[41] The head of Jackson's column had covered, at best, four miles during the past four hours, and only seven miles since dawn.

The ensuing desultory, though often bitter, engagement lasted until nightfall and became known as the battle of Chantilly or Ox Hill, names that somewhat obscure the significance of the fighting. Both Chantilly and Ox Hill are about six miles from the junction of the Little River Turnpike and the road from Centreville. The search for these two locales on a map, such as the one published in Douglas Southall Freeman's *Lee's Lieutenants*, would lead a reader to believe that Jackson's march had fallen well short of its objective.[42] But the battle was actually fought about three miles further along the pike just to the east of the Ox Road. McDowell reported that when the leading elements of his corps reached Germantown they moved forward along the turnpike and checked the Confederate advance along Difficult Creek, which flows at right angles to the pike just east of Ox Road. Major General Jesse Reno's troops came up and struck Jackson's flank about 5:50 P.M.[43]

Jackson was within three miles of his objective—the retreat route of Pope's army—which explains the stiffening Federal resistance.[44] The fighting was at close quarters as a stiff wind drove a cold rain into the faces of the advancing Rebels. Lightning flashed overhead and the boom of thunder replaced that of the cannon; guns could rarely find clear fields of fire in the heavily broken and wooded terrain. On occasion, wet powder forced commanders to resort to the melee. Two Federal division commanders fell amidst the confused fighting.

But despite the chaos and the hard—and at times desperate—nature of the engagement, Jackson's casualties were light—

about five hundred—and the bulk of his command never took part in the battle. Nor did the troops of Lee's right wing. When Longstreet reached the field of battle, he sought out Jackson only to find the general observing men from one of his regiments heading toward the rear.

"General," Longstreet remarked, "your men don't appear to work well to-day."

"No," Jackson replied, "but I hope it will prove a victory in the morning."[45]

But there would be no continuation of the battle the next day. Pope was retreating, a movement promptly reported by Stuart's cavalry patrols. Since the network of roads did not lend itself to yet another effort to outflank the Army of Virginia, Lee knew that the campaign against Pope's army was over.

A DETAILED REVIEW of the extant and readily available documentation reveals that those who have attributed Jackson's failure to reach Fairfax Court House to a combination of bad roads, foul weather, tired troops, and some spirited Federal resistance are in error.[46] There can be little doubt that by the time A. P. Hill's division went forward about 4:00 P.M. Jackson had little chance to cut Pope's line of retreat. The better part of three Federal corps were at or moving toward Fairfax Court House. Given the lateness of the day, the deteriorating weather, the terrain, and the evident fact that Beverly Robertson had failed to cover the right flank of the advance, Jackson had every reason not to press his attack. But if Jackson seriously intended to force his army into Pope's rear, Stonewall should, and could, have reached the intersection of the Ox Road and Little River Turnpike well before 4:00 P.M. His troops marched an average of a mile and a half an hour in the rain over the country road on the thirty-first, a slow pace for the "foot cavalry" of the Valley army. Had Jackson's men maintained that rate of march along the turnpike on September 1, they would have reached Ox Road between 10:00 and 11:00 A.M. Pope did not order McDowell to Fairfax Court House until noon.

Why had Jackson's column moved so slowly? The weather did not break until the late afternoon and was better, not worse, than it had been the previous day—hence the dust clouds thrown up by Longstreet's troops, visible from the Federal positions west of Centreville. There can be no comparison between the difficult country road Jackson's men navigated on August 31 and the Little River Turnpike—a stretch of highway broad enough to accommodate files of infantry on either side with enough road left over in the center for artillery columns.[47] Jackson's troops were, without a doubt, tired. They had had a morning's rest on the day after Second Manassas, but a difficult march that afternoon. Jackson's footsore soldiers had spent the night of August 31–September 1 in an open, rain-soaked field, reportedly without rations—hardly a recipe for a recovery of strength.[48] Nevertheless, according to an account written by one Rebel soldier, the delays were the fault of the officers, and not the rank and file. "The officers high in authority," William A. McClendan wrote, "didn't seem to be in any great hurry."[49] Nor was McClendan's regiment short of rations. They still carried supplies that had been issued before Second Manassas and, in the meantime, had "access to the well-filled haversacks of the dead boys in blue, so that there was nothing short in the ration department." Could Jackson, with the rear of Pope's army exposed, not have extolled his men to do more than meander along the turnpike averaging little better than a half-mile an hour? The men of Major General Richard S. Ewell's division moved with Longstreet's wing and began their trek later on August 31, but marched throughout the night until they, too, reached the turnpike. Despite the fact that Ewell's men had less rest, slept under the same skies, and feasted on the same rations, Brigadier General Jubal A. Early, who was in temporary command of the division, had his men on the march early the next morning.[50]

But not Jackson. Was Stonewall displaying the uncertainty and hesitation that had afflicted him during the Seven Days' campaign? Did he simply allow an opportunity to slip through his fingers?[51] Was he concerned about placing his already battered brigades into yet another exposed position where they would bear the brunt of any Federal assault? Or was Jackson's mind fixed on the Potomac, and not another march around John Pope's flank? This last interpretation would explain the relative celerity with which Jackson marched north—toward the Potomac—on August 31, and the lack of speed he demonstrated while moving toward the southeast—away from the river—on September 1. The memoir of Heros von Borcke, who was at Stuart's side during his two meetings with Jackson on the first, suggests that neither Jackson nor Lee were as determined as they might have been to find a way around Pope's flank. Von Borcke's portrait of Jackson, observing his sharpshooters at play and then waiting until noon to order Stuart beyond Chantilly, is not one of an aggressive commander gripped by any sense of urgency to push his troops toward their objective. As von Borcke noted: "Our Generals . . . did not suppose that [the Federals] really intended to make a stand at that point, and their further retreat towards Alexandria was confidently expected."[52] According to von Borcke's understanding of the situation, Lee, in fact, "did not deem it advisable to press [the Federals] vigourously."[53] Lee and Jackson, having assumed that Pope would promptly retreat, failed to take advantage of the situation as it developed on September 1, for their gaze was already fixed on the Potomac River.

WHATEVER THE CAUSE of the failure of the flank march, Lee immediately set a new plan into action, one that would carry the army to the banks of, and in all probability across, the Potomac River. That very night—September 1, 1862—Jeb Stuart ordered Colonel Thomas T. Munford to move with his Second Virginia Cavalry from his position near the Ox Road to Leesburg. Munford's orders directed him to drive a small force of Yankee irregulars, little more than a collection of "notorious ruffians" commanded by Captain Samuel P. Means, from the town, which the colonel succeeded in doing the next day. [54]

While Munford's march no doubt saved the citizens of Leesburg from further harassment, the principal reason for the detachment of the Second Virginia was to clear the town of Federal troops as a prelude to a possible crossing of the Potomac. Lee also dispatched one of his commissary officers, Major B. P. Nolan, to join Munford and to organize the roundup of cattle to feed the army.[55] Hours before Munford's men reached their objective, Lee dictated orders for D. H. Hill to march his division north toward Dranesville, where he was to pick up the Leesburg Pike and follow that road west to Leesburg.[56] Later that same day Lee directed Longstreet to fall in behind Hill.[57] Jackson's men would resume their march early on the morning of the third.

During the night of the first or the morning of the second, Lee conferred with Jackson about the prospects of a move across the Potomac. Jackson had long advocated an invasion of the North and was eager to carry the war into Maryland.[58] But the two men differed on the question of where the army ought to cross the river. Jackson proposed that the march through Leesburg continue along the turnpike into the Shenandoah Valley and that Lee clear Federal forces from Winchester and Harpers Ferry before passing over the Potomac.[59] Lee feared that a movement so far removed from Washington would fail to induce the Federals to cross over to the north bank of the river. Lee believed that a crossing at the fords around Leesburg, midway between Washington and Harpers Ferry, would compel the Federals to bring their main army over to the north bank and to abandon both Winchester and Harpers Ferry. Lee rejected Jackson's advice.

Later that day or the next, Lee discussed his plans with Longstreet as the two generals rode together toward Leesburg. Longstreet's strategic and operational views frequently diverged from those of his commander in chief, but not with regard to the invasion of Maryland. Longstreet enthusiastically supported the decision to cross the Potomac. When Lee expressed doubt about his ability to supply the army, Longstreet, as he later wrote, dismissed such concerns:

> I related my Mexican War experiences with Worth's division, marching around the city of Monterey on two-days' rations of roasting ears and green oranges, and said that it seemed to me that we could trust to the fields of Maryland, laden with ripening corn and fruit, to do as much as those of Mexico; that we could in fact subsist on the bounty of the fields until we could open communication with our organized base of supply.[60]

While Lee had set his army in motion toward Leesburg, he was still not irrevocably committed to crossing the river, there or anywhere. The army could continue its march along the pike to Winchester and operate in the Valley, either in an effort to clear the Shenandoah of enemy troops or as a prelude to a Potomac crossing at Harpers Ferry. On September 2, Lee, perhaps still uncertain as to his future course of action, drafted the first of a series of letters to President Jefferson Davis.[61]

Lee, his hands too sore to write, dictated the letter to his military secretary, Major A. L. Long. "The present seems to be the most propitious time since the commencement of the war," Lee explained, "for the Confederate Army to enter Maryland." Continued pursuit of Pope was pointless. An invasion might "afford" the Marylanders "an opportunity of throwing off" Federal "oppression." The Federal armies were "much weakened and demoralized." Their ranks were thinned and the inevitable replacements available, but not yet trained. A march into Loudon County would allow the commissary corps to gather supplies while the central position of the army would menace both Washington and the Shenandoah Valley. And then, "if practicable," Lee could "cross into Maryland." "The purpose, if discovered," Long scribbled as Lee continued to dictate, "will have the effect of carrying the enemy north of the Potomac, and, if prevented, will not result in much evil." Lee admitted that his army was "not properly equipped for an invasion of an enemy's territory." Every kind of supply, even the most basic items such as shoes, was lacking. "Still," Lee believed, "we cannot afford to be idle, and though weaker than our opponents in men and military equipments, must endeavor to harass if we cannot destroy them. I am aware that the movement is attended with much risk, yet I do not consider success impossible, and shall endeavor to guard it from loss." Lee also suggested to Davis that if the army of General Braxton Bragg could not "operate to advantage on its present frontier" in Tennessee, the bulk of it should be transferred to Virginia.[62]

While Long completed the draft on the second, the letter that ultimately reached Richmond was addressed from "Near Dranesville, September 3, 1862."[63] The hesitant tone of the message, combined with the change of date, could indicate that Lee was uncertain about his plans and, as of the second, unsure whether he wished to raise the question of an invasion with the Confederate president. But the delay could also indicate that the general wished to ensure that Davis could not interfere with the operations of the Army of Northern Virginia.

It was in this latter spirit that Lee wrote again on the fourth, this time from Leesburg, announcing his determination to cross the Potomac.[64] "I shall proceed to make the movement at once," he advised the president, "unless you should signify your disapprobation"—an impossibility considering the fact that Davis was 120 miles away in Richmond and no working telegraph linked Leesburg and the Confederate capital. The supposedly hesitant Lee now spoke of marching through Maryland and into Pennsylvania. He assured the president that the crossing would bring not just Pope and McClellan to the north bank of the Potomac, but also leave "the Valley entirely free." Lee admitted that the supply of the army would be tenuous, but was convinced that such difficulties could be overcome.

Lee's letter of September 4 is a remarkable and disingenuous document. Here we have the commander of one of the most important of the Confederate armies about to undertake a risky invasion of northern territory on his own initiative.[65] The argument has been made that Lee knew that Davis would approve the decision. If so, then why not state such an assumed approval in the letter instead of requesting of the president some signal of "disapprobation" impossible to make, given the fact that the lead elements of D. H. Hill's division were but hours from their scheduled crossings? Lee knew that it was physically impossible for Davis to even receive, let alone reply to, the letter before the army was across the Potomac and into Maryland. For example, letters Lee sent to Secretary of War George W. Randolph on September 2 and 3 reached Richmond on September 6 and 8, respectively. Perhaps the delay in sending the letter of September 2 was indicative not of Lee's hesitation, but of his determination to keep his intentions secret from his civilian commander in chief in Richmond? As Longstreet recalled after the war: "[Lee's] early experiences with the Richmond authorities taught him to deal cautiously with them in disclosing his views, and to leave for them the privilege and credit of approving, step by step, his apparently hesitant policy, so that his plans were disclosed little at a time."[66]

On September 5, Lee wrote yet another letter to Davis, again from Leesburg.[67] Lee reiterated many of the points he had made in his previous dispatches. He wrote of "liberating" the people of Maryland and of his intention to "annoy and harass" the Federals. But Lee also informed Davis that the army would shift its line of communications to the Shenandoah Valley and abandon the one running back through Manassas, Warrenton, Culpeper, and Gordonsville. Lee's movements since September 1 had implied such a shift, whether or not the army actually passed over the Potomac. But only now, as Jackson's and Longstreet's troops entered Maryland, did Lee either recognize, or choose to acknowledge to the president, that the invasion placed at risk an incredible haul of matériel abandoned by Pope's army around Manassas. Just how much booty was involved is uncertain. The soldiers of the Army of Northern Virginia had already helped themselves to the artillery, rifled muskets, supplies of food and clothing, shoes, and wagons left behind by the retreating Federals. But much else remained on the battlefield. Lee mentioned a stand of ten to twelve thousand arms at Gainesville and an unspecified number of "locomotives and cars" captured at Bristoe and Manassas.[68] By the time Davis learned that Lee would no longer be relying on or covering his old line of communications, it was too late to act. Lee later lamented that the bulk of these resources were destroyed by the Confederates themselves, to prevent recapture, and by raiding Federal forces. Had Lee been more forthright in his communications with Davis, perhaps some of this invaluable material could have been recovered for use by the Confederate States.

Despite Lee's fears, greater honesty in his communications with the president would probably not have prompted Davis to direct Lee to remain south of the Potomac. Lee's victories had gained him the initiative, not only on the field of maneuver, but also in his dealings with his political superiors in Richmond. Davis was hardly in a position to suddenly shorten the leash on his most successful general. Moreover, there existed in the Confederate capital, and more broadly throughout the Confederacy, a consensus in support of a policy of invasion. As a September 6 editorial in the *Charleston Mercury* noted: "Our victorious troops in Virginia, reduced though they be in numbers, and shattered in organization, must be led promptly into Maryland, before the enemy can rally the masses of recruits whom he is rapidly and steadily gathering together."[69] Lee was one of many Southerners caught up in a wave of "victory disease," not unlike that which gripped the Japanese before the battle of Midway.[70] Even the historian writing more than a century after the event, possessing full knowledge of the mishaps about to befall the Army of Northern Virginia, can only with difficulty conclude that the Maryland campaign should never have been undertaken.

But the facts remain: in shaping national strategy on the march, Lee exceeded his responsibilities as army commander.

Lee was neither timely nor forthright in his communications with Jefferson Davis. And the president of the Confederacy was not alone in his ignorance of Lee's plans; some of the general's principal subordinates were less than fully informed about their commander's intentions. As one Virginia soldier wrote:

> . . . a thousand rumors as to the whereabouts of the enemy and as many speculations as to our destination some say Baltimore others say Pennsylvania. No one knows not even the Brgd. Generals. They are just as ignorant in this respect as privates. Jackson and Lee keep there own secrets and I have perfect confidence in them. They will be at the right place at the right time.[71]

But they would not be!

In an effort to explain the decision to invade Maryland, Douglas Southall Freeman, Lee's most prominent biographer, reviewed the general's 1862 correspondence with Davis, the official report written in March 1863, and several postwar comments and letters. Freeman concluded that there was "remarkable consistency among these accounts, though the last was written six and a half years after the first."[72] And the accounts cited by Freeman are consistent: in each Lee stated that his intention was to feed his army on Northern soil and to forestall a renewed invasion of Virginia until the campaigning season was over.

Lee apparently offered similar explanations to his subordinates. Longstreet, who published his memoirs decades after the war, wrote that the army was "obliged to go into Maryland or retreat to points more convenient to supplies and the protection of Richmond."[73] Brigadier General John G. Walker, whose division joined the army shortly after it crossed into Maryland, reported to Lee at Frederick. According to Walker's postwar account, Lee informed his division commander that since he was to operate detached, he "might require a knowledge of the ulterior purposes and objects of the campaign."[74] Lee then outlined, as one must assume he had done for his other senior officers, the broad scope of his plan of campaign. Again, the themes were feeding the army and harassing the Federals. Lee informed Walker that "a few days rest" in the western Maryland countryside would revive the army's strength. New recruits would arrive. Stragglers would rejoin their units. Then "tracing his finger on a large map," Lee sketched out his planned operations in western Maryland and south central Pennsylvania, including the major objective: a move to Harrisburg to destroy the great railroad bridge over the Susquehanna River. As the "astonished" Walker wondered about the prospect of some countermove by McClellan, Lee remarked that the Federal commander was "an able general but a very cautious one" who would not undertake any offensive action for three or four weeks.

Noticeably absent from these accounts was any mention of battle. This is remarkable, considering that ever since taking command of the army in June, Lee had incessantly sought battle in an effort to destroy first McClellan and later Pope. Had Lee suddenly lost his faith in the ability of battle to produce decision?

The history of Lee's subsequent campaigns hardly supports the suggestion that after Second Manassas the commander of the Army of Northern Virginia eschewed the centrality of battle in his plans of operations. Unless Lee had undergone some dramatic, albeit temporary, transformation, he entered Maryland in early September 1862 fully prepared to fight, and hopefully to fight the decisive battle on Northern soil.

Robert Dabney, who served on Jackson's staff and whose memoir provides some insight into the mind of Stonewall Jackson, likewise cited the usual advantages of carrying the war north of the Potomac. But in Dabney's account, the prospect of battle remained central to the proposed campaign. Lee, Dabney wrote, hoped that the Federal army "might be defeated upon their own soil, and a successful incursion might carry a wholesome terror into the heart of Pennsylvania."[75]

Two recently published postwar accounts support this view. In February 1868 Lee had frank discussions about the war with William Allan and Edward Clifton Gordon at Washington

College.[76] Lee usually refrained from discussing his wartime experiences and rarely offered criticism of his former subordinates, but the publication of a self-serving account of the Maryland campaign by Daniel Harvey Hill so outraged Lee that he temporarily shed his usual reticence.

In his discussion with Allan, Lee, at first, offered the standard explanations for the Maryland campaign. He spoke of the need "to relieve Va. from both armies" and "to live for a time on the abundant supplies in Maryland."[77] But as he reviewed his moves and countermoves, he expressed regret that McClellan had not delayed long enough to allow the reconcentration of the Army of Northern Virginia. If he had, Lee told Allan, "I *intended then to attack McClellan*, hoping the best results from state of my troops & those of the enemy."[78]

In a conversation later that same day with Gordon, Lee was even more animated. As he spoke he became " . . . excited, & somewhat indignant with Gen. Hill" and contemptuous of McClellan. And then, with his eyes "flashing," Lee told Gordon: "I went into Maryland to give battle, and could I have kept Gen. McClelland [*sic*] in ignorance of my position & plans a day or two longer, I would have fought and crushed him."[79]

Lee's decision to cross the Potomac into Maryland was probably the worst he ever made as a general. He was about to undertake a major offensive operation into Federal territory, the military and political ramifications of which were enormous, without discussing the matter, or at least the timing, with President Davis. Despite the extraordinary nature of the undertaking, no logistical forethought had been given to the expedition. There was no plan of operations, except for whatever existed in Lee's and Jackson's heads. Of the army's major commanders, only Stonewall fully understood Lee's mind. The extant documentation clearly indicates that Longstreet learned that the army would cross the Potomac just as he had learned of the planned flank march to Chantilly: after Lee and Jackson had conferred privately and reached a decision.

AS STUART'S CAVALRY covered Lee's rear with screens and a demonstration toward Alexandria, the Army of Northern Virginia's units began crossing the Potomac at the fords near Leesburg on September 4 and 5, 1862.[80] D. H. Hill's division, after crossing at White's Ford, formed the van on the roads leading north.

For Lee, still nursing his injured wrists, the march from the Potomac to Frederick, Maryland, may have been the high point of his war. He sensed that the conflict was about to reach a climax. The prospects for a successful campaign in Maryland appeared favorable. In fact, the entire course of the war seemed to have taken a turn in the favor of the Confederacy. On September 6 Lee received news of Major General E. Kirby Smith's victory at Richmond, Kentucky.[81] Obviously exhilarated by the news, Lee issued a general order to the army:

> The general commanding takes pleasure in announcing to the brave soldiers of the Army of Northern Virginia the signal success of their comrades in arms in the West. The Confederate forces, under the command of Maj. Gen. E. Kirby Smith, defeated on August 30 the Federal forces commanded by General Nelson, capturing General Nelson and his staff, 3,000 prisoners, and all his artillery, small-arms, wagons, &c. This great victory is simultaneous with your own at Manassas. Soldiers, press onward! Let each man feel the responsibility now resting on him to pursue vigorously the success vouchsafed to us by Heaven. Let the armies of the East and the West vie with each other in discipline, bravery, and activity, and our brethren of our sister States will soon be released from tyranny, and our independence be established upon a sure and abiding basis.[82]

Lee's ebullience filtered down through his staff. On the seventh, Major Walter H. Taylor wrote that the army was "in fine trim and spirits," busily acquiring its needs from the Marylanders. "Just now," Taylor wrote, "it does appear as if God was truly with us."[83]

The next day Lee, from his headquarters outside Frederick, wrote President Davis suggesting that the moment had arrived for the "Government of the Confederate States to propose with propriety to that of the United States the recognition of our independence." Lee expected that if such a move did not result in an immediate termination of the war, it would have positive diplomatic ramifications and would also "enable the people of the United States to determine at their coming elections whether they will support those who favor a prolongation of the war, or those who wish to bring it to a termination, which can but be productive of good to both parties without affecting the honor of either."[84]

But Lee's plans for the campaign were already unraveling. Despite Taylor's comments about the state of the army, straggling and desertion had become a major problem. A. J. Dula, who served in a North Carolina regiment, recalled that even "good soldiers would straggle, so many were barefooted, ragged and foot sore and partly sick and worn out by constant travel."[85] Another North Carolina soldier claimed that someone had, in fact, issued an "order excusing bare-footed men from marching into Maryland."[86] While this was obviously nothing more than a rumor, it nevertheless sent thousands to the rear. On September 6 Lee, in an effort to stop this veritable hemorrhaging of the army's manpower, belatedly appointed Brigadier General Lewis A. Armistead as provost marshal, giving him the "authority to call for guards, take all proper measures to correct irregularities against good order and military discipline, and prevent depredations upon the community."[87]

On the seventh, Lee dispatched two letters to the capital for the president. The first was rather positive, noting with some degree of exaggeration that the army was being well received in Maryland.[88] But in the second letter Lee noted that the usual lax discipline of the army had "not been improved by the forced marches and hard service" of the present campaign. He wrote:

One of the greatest evils, from which many minor ones proceed, is the habit of straggling from the ranks. The higher officers feel as I do, and I believe have done all in their power to stop it. It has become a habit difficult to correct. With some, the sick and feeble, it results from necessity, but with the greater number from design. These latter do not wish to be with their regiments, nor to share in their hardships and glories. They are the cowards of the army, desert their comrades in times of danger, and fill the houses of the charitable and hospitable in the march.[89]

On the ninth, only four days after the army's crossing of the Potomac, Lee's letters to Davis began to reflect a serious and growing concern about the course of the campaign. Lee now admitted that the people of western Maryland were far less cooperative than he had hoped. Many were unwilling to accept Confederate currency as payment; others were driving their livestock northward into Pennsylvania. As one Confederate veteran later recalled, many of the soldiers believed that "Lee's usual foresight and sagacity failed him that pop, certain," since he had made a mistake by "starting off with us before the corn was fit to eat."[90] Worse yet, reports from Stuart's cavalry, which had finally caught up with the army, indicated that the Federals were already on the move, far earlier than Lee expected. The van of McClellan's army had passed through Rockville and was across the Seneca Creek, reaching toward Poolesville, a town midway and eighteen miles between Washington and Frederick.[91] Lee faced the prospect of battle with Harpers Ferry, in Federal hands, in his rear.

Later that day Lee, recognizing that his original plan of campaign had gone awry, conferred with Jackson. Stonewall suggested that Lee ignore Harpers Ferry, keep the army concentrated around Frederick, and "fight McClellan as he advanced."[92] But Lee favored an alternative plan. He would march the army to the west, place South Mountain between him and the Federals, have Jackson recross the river to secure

Harpers Ferry, and then reconcentrate the army on the north bank of the Potomac. According to Dabney, Jackson argued that Lee's plan was "too complex for realizing that punctual and complete concentration which sound policy required."[93] As he had at Chantilly, Lee rejected his subordinate's advice.

Interestingly, Lee had taken yet another major decision without conferring with the commander of his other wing. On the afternoon of the ninth Longstreet, well aware of the crisis facing the army, called upon his commander but, as he later wrote, "found the front of the general's tent closed and tied." A member of the headquarters staff informed Longstreet that Lee was inside meeting with Jackson. "As I had not been called," Longstreet recalled, "I turned to go away, when General Lee, recognizing my voice, called me in. The plan had been arranged."[94]

Later that day Lee dictated Special Order 191, the first, and last, substantive planning document he had yet issued during the campaign. The Army of Northern Virginia would shift its base to the northwest, toward Hagerstown. Jackson would re-cross the Potomac and seize Harpers Ferry by September 15, securing a line of communications into the Shenandoah Valley. Stuart and D. H. Hill would form the rear guard and cover the passes through South Mountain. As soon as possible, the army would reconcentrate north of the river.

On September 10, Lee's army was once again on the move. The Confederates entered Hagerstown on the twelfth, from where Lee wrote the president explaining the reasons for the sudden change of plan. Lee was now playing for time with his army divided into four separate groups. From Hagerstown he urged his subordinates to complete their operations with all haste so that the army could reconcentrate before the Federals struck.

AS GEORGE B. McCLELLAN BREAKFASTED on the morning of September 2, two guests made a surprise appearance at his headquarters—President Lincoln and General Halleck. With the army in retreat and the Federal capital threatened, Lincoln had decided to place McClellan in charge. As Pope's army withdrew back to the environs of Washington, his troops would pass to McClellan's command.[95]

McClellan, once again in command of the army opposing Lee, now faced a difficult task. He had to meld simultaneously two defeated armies—his own Army of the Potomac, beaten in the Peninsula, and Pope's Army of Virginia, recently bested at Second Manassas—into a single force capable of opposing what appeared to be a massive and dangerous Confederate invasion of the north.

Even before the engagement at Chantilly, McClellan had suspected that Lee would make a move across the Potomac west of the capital. The new Federal commander hoped to quickly concentrate his army north of the river and strike Lee's flank as he crossed.[96] Unfortunately, accurate intelligence about the strength and location of Lee's army, well screened by Stuart's troopers, was difficult to obtain. Reports indicated that Lee had as many as one hundred thousand men, nearly three times the actual strength of the Army of Northern Virginia. Nor was it clear that his entire force had crossed the river. The possibility existed that the units on the north bank were conducting a feint meant to lure the Federals away from Washington. No doubt the thousands of Confederate stragglers and deserters roaming about the countryside both north and south of the river made it appear as if Lee commanded a vast horde footloose in northern Virginia and western Maryland.[97]

McClellan's uncertainty resulted in what were initially cautious countermoves toward the west along the north bank of the Potomac. Nevertheless, McClellan's marches were sudden enough to upset Lee's original plan, based as it was on an assumption that weeks would pass before the Federals would make any substantive response. On September 4, as Lee's troops crossed the Potomac, McClellan already had the van of his army on the Rockville Road marching for Poolesville.[98] By the eighth, McClellan was confident that Washington and Baltimore were safe. On the afternoon of September 9 McClellan, though still uncertain about Lee's movements, began to shift his army further forward.[99] Over the next forty-eight hours, McClellan concluded that Lee's move was not a feint and that the entire Confederate army was across the Potomac, although with as many as 120,000 men. What McClellan did not understand was why Lee appeared to be moving toward the south and west, rather than the north and east.

On September 12 McClellan ordered a general advance toward Frederick. The latest reports to reach his headquarters indicated that the Confederates had abandoned the town and perhaps were already "skedadelling." He wrote his wife: "I begin to think that he is making off to get out of the scrape by recrossing the river at Williamsport. . . . He evidently dont' want to fight me—for some reason or another."[100] If his forward movement did not result in battle, McClellan at least hoped that it might save the garrison at Harpers Ferry. He had favored the evacuation of the town, but Halleck, who placed the troops under McClellan's control only that morning, had demurred. Unfortunately for the Federals, the fate of the Harpers Ferry garrison was already sealed.

Late on the afternoon of September 12, Union troops entered Frederick. McClellan established his new headquarters in the town, and it was there, on the morning of the thirteenth, that he received a copy of Lee's Special Order 191, discovered by two Yankee soldiers in an abandoned Confederate encampment.

While the oft-debated responsibility for the "Lost Dispatch" is irrelevant to the story here, the same is not true of the question of the significance of the dispatch to the course of the campaign. Douglas Southall Freeman argued that "the unsuccessful outcome of the operations in Maryland will be found to hinge upon the unexpected rapidity and assurance of the Federal movements on and after September 13."[101] There can be no doubt that McClellan, once in possession of Lee's orders, was more certain in his movements. Nevertheless, the fact remains that McClellan had reached Frederick, forty-five miles from Washington and only fifteen from Antietam Creek, *before* the discovery of the dispatch. McClellan did not advance because his troops stumbled across the dispatch; his troops discovered the dispatch because McClellan was already advancing.[102] McClellan's earlier than expected reaction had checked Lee's original plan of campaign long before September 13.

The possession of the Lost Dispatch offered McClellan the opportunity to do more than simply to counter Lee's Northern invasion; McClellan now had a chance to destroy Lee's army in battle. At noon on the thirteenth McClellan wrote Lincoln:

> I have the whole rebel force in front of me, but am confident, and no time shall be lost. I have a difficult task to perform, but with God's blessing will accomplish it. I think Lee has made a gross mistake, and that he will be severely punished for it. The army is in motion as rapidly as possible. I hope for a great success if the plans of the rebels remain unchallenged. We have possession of Catoctin. I have all the plans of the rebels, and will catch them in their own trap if my men are equal to the emergency. I now feel that I can count on them as of old. All forces of Pennsylvania should be placed to cooperate at Chambersburg. My respects to Mrs. Lincoln. Received most enthusiastically by the ladies. Will send you trophies. All well, and with God's blessing will accomplish it.[103]

On the fourteenth, as McClellan's van fought its way through Crampton's and Turner's Gaps, breaching the Confederate position on South Mountain, Lee found himself facing disaster. A general who only a few days before had believed that his movements might force an end to the war was now fighting for survival. With his army divided and weakened by desertion, its strength unknown even to its commander, Lee ordered a reconcentration at Sharpsburg, from where he could escape across the Potomac to Virginia, and safety.[104] But as the tired regiments of the Army of Northern Virginia gathered west of Antietam Creek, Lee received a message from Jackson: Harpers Ferry would fall by the next day.[105] Lee now reversed himself: there would be no retreat. He dispatched orders to his detached units to hasten their march to Sharpsburg as soon as Harpers Ferry surrendered. Lee—heavily outnumbered, his force still divided, and with his back to a river—had decided to fight.[106]

Lee's decision has puzzled historians, for the likelihood of defeat, at least in retrospect, seems to have outweighed the prospects of success.[107] Lee's plan to roam about the Northern countryside had already and quite obviously failed. Nor did Lee have to fight to extract his army from Maryland. Half of his men were already across the Potomac, and the rest could have crossed at Sharpsburg without interference. That being the case, why risk battle? The answer is simple: because it was battle that Lee had sought when he first crossed the Potomac. As Robert Dabney of Jackson's staff wrote:

> The battle of Sharpsburg was fought by the Confederates not to purchase a secure retreat, but to open their way for a triumphant invasion; to redeem their offers of aid to oppressed Maryland; to conquer a peace by defeating the oppressors upon their own soil. This truth displays at once the daring and hardihood of General Lee's conceptions, and his confidence in the prowess of his army. He believed them capable of everything, and so was not afraid to require of them the greatest things.[108]

McClellan's faster than expected response had restricted Lee's movements, but had not lessened the likelihood of battle, albeit now under disadvantageous circumstances. But since Lee had crossed the Potomac in search of battle, he was not prepared to recross it without having fought one. He was confident, as he watched the Federal troops arriving along the Antietam on the afternoon of September 15, that McClellan would not attack until the seventeenth, by which time Lee expected to have reconcentrated his army.[109] Nor was the Sharpsburg position weak. To be sure, Lee was heavily outnumbered and his back was to a river, but that same river protected the Confederate flanks against an envelopment by McClellan's larger force. The Antietam Creek, passable at only a few points, likewise constricted any possible Federal advance and allowed Lee to economize his force—that is, to hold off much larger Federal forces with a veritable handful of troops.

To defeat Lee, McClellan had to make the most of his numerical superiority by launching a series of simultaneous frontal blows against the Confederate line. Such assaults would be costly, but offered the best hope of overwhelming Lee's hard-pressed army.

Unfortunately for the Federals, while McClellan's administration of the army and maneuvers in western Maryland had bested Lee strategically and operationally, the Federal commander in chief proved himself a tactical incompetent. The Army of the Potomac wasted much of the sixteenth getting into position. When the assault began on the morning of September 17, the Federal corps entered the battle piecemeal. McClellan attacked first with his right, then with his left, and only late in the day with his center. The Federal commander, convinced that Lee possessed "great odds against me," fought cautiously, waiting to see how his "flank movements . . . developed."[110] As a result, each Federal assault nearly shattered the Confederate lines, but Lee was able to counter the successive attacks with his reserves until late in the afternoon when A. P. Hill reached the battlefield with his famous Light Division and drove back the Yankee troops threatening Sharpsburg.

The next day, the two tired and battered armies remained in place, each commander expecting, if not hoping, his opponent to renew the assault. But, except for some skirmishing, the battle was over. On the evening of September 18, Lee recrossed the Potomac. McClellan, having gained ground during the fighting on the seventeenth, declared himself the victor. "Last night," he wrote Halleck on September 19, "the enemy abandoned his position leaving his dead & wounded on the field. . . . We may safely claim a complete victory."[111]

DESPITE McCLELLAN'S CLAIM, Douglas Southall Freeman, Lee's best-known biographer, considered the Maryland campaign a marked Confederate success. Lee's army suffered over thirteen thousand casualties during the course of the entire campaign, including twelve thousand at Antietam, or Sharpsburg as the Rebels called the battle. The Federals themselves lost twelve thousand along Antietam Creek, making September 17, 1862, the bloodiest day in American military history. However, the Union forces suffered additional losses of fifteen thousand men in assorted skirmishes and, most importantly, in the capture of the garrison at Harpers Ferry. Thus, the twenty-seven thousand Federal losses were more than double those suffered by the army of Robert E. Lee, the true victor of the Maryland campaign.

But more important than any juxtaposition of casualty lists is a comparison of the course of the campaign with Lee's objectives, stated and otherwise. And here his effort must be judged an abject failure. Lee marched into Maryland to carry the war to the North, or so he said. But Lee carried the war into one rather small corner of Northern territory and stayed there, at great risk, for a mere fortnight—from the fourth through the eighteenth of September. As Walter Taylor of Lee's staff noted in a September 21 letter to his sister, "I suppose it will be generally concluded that our march through—or rather into—Maryland & back was decidedly meteoric."[112] Nor did Lee achieve his principal, if unstated, goal of the campaign: He did not win a major victory on Federal soil. While Sharpsburg was a draw— or perhaps, arguably, a Confederate tactical victory—it was, relatively speaking, a veritable Federal triumph when compared to the disasters that had befallen Union armies at Second Manassas or during the battles of the Peninsula campaign. Robert E. Lee had not invaded Maryland to fight a stalemated engagement with his back to a river to be followed by a withdrawal into the Shenandoah Valley. Lee, who had expected that his campaign and battlefield success north of the Potomac would have a serious political and diplomatic impact on the course of the war, perhaps even forcing its end, instead threw away the fruits of his summer triumphs in a gamble, the failure of which permitted the Lincoln administration to solidify its political support and, by avoiding another military debacle and through issuance of the Emancipation Proclamation, to strengthen its diplomatic position.

Why had Lee failed? The answer is simple: virtually all of the assumptions upon which he based his plans were unfounded.

Lee assumed that the people of western Maryland would welcome and support a Confederate invasion, but the population reacted cautiously and to an extent with outright hostility when faced with the Rebel presence. Recruits for the army were few and supplies remained difficult to acquire. The troops who had forded the Potomac with their bands playing "Maryland, My Maryland" quickly developed a particular distaste for the tune. As Walter Taylor noted, after the army's return to Virginia "one of the bands commenced the air . . . & was prevented from proceeding by the groans & hisses of the soldiers."[113]

Lee assumed that the Federals would abandon their positions in the Shenandoah Valley without a fight, thus securing the valley route for a new Confederate line of communications. But the Federals stubbornly, if unwisely, refused to evacuate Harpers Ferry, prompting Lee to divide his army in an effort to clear his rear.

Nor was Lee's assumption correct that control of Harpers Ferry was a prerequisite for a secure line of supply through the valley. As the summer campaign of 1863 would demonstrate, the garrison at Harpers Ferry could have been contained—or screened—by a small force; there was no need to take the town by siege or assault.

Lee assumed that his army, despite the past several grueling months of marching and fighting, would hold together if he carried it into Maryland. Instead, the army suffered from massive desertion. Lee clearly expected far too much from his men and failed to foresee the impact of straggling on the army, a factor that, by his own admission, may have cost him as many as half of his troops. As Martin van Creveld wrote in *Command in War,* a general in chief bears two principal and interrelated responsibilities. First, he must "arrange and coordinate everything an army needs to exist—its food supply, its sanitary service, its system of military justice, and so on."[114] Second, that army must "carry out its proper mission, which is to inflict the maximum amount of death and destruction on the enemy within the shortest possible period of time and at minimum loss to itself . . ." In the preindustrial age the former function of command—keeping an army intact in the field—was an extremely difficult challenge, and in that sense a primary task. What, then, can be said of a general who not only lost one-third to one-half of his army to desertion, but also was unsure of just how many men were actually missing on the eve of what was going to be a desperate battle, and who had taken little preemptive action to forestall such a disaster? The scope of the straggling is understandable, given the conditions facing the Rebel soldiers. Lee's army was, to be sure, woefully undersupplied. But Lee knew full well that his troops had been poorly fed, clothed, and supplied when operating in Virginia. Nor can one fault the Confederate government and quartermaster corps for failing to support a major offensive that Lee launched on his own initiative while purposefully keeping his decision to cross to the north bank of the Potomac and switching his lines of communication to the valley from the president of the Confederate States government.

If Lee had overestimated the prowess of his own troops, he was also guilty of underestimating his opponents—both McClellan and the Army of the Potomac. Lee expected the Federals to respond slowly to the Rebel invasion, providing him with ample time to fatten up and strengthen his army before facing the prospect of battle. Unfortunately for the Confederates, McClellan moved with relative celerity, well before the discovery of the infamous Lost Dispatch, and began to complicate Lee's operations less than a week after he had crossed the Potomac. As late as September 8, Lee assured Walker at Frederick that McClellan would not go over to the offensive for three to four weeks, during which the Confederates would be free to forage amongst the friendly people of western Maryland, perhaps even raiding as far afield as Pennsylvania. Because Lee led his advance across the Potomac with his infantry, and assigned to Stuart the role of rear guard, the army was well into Maryland before the cavalry could reach its proper position in the van and on the flanks. As a result, the movements of McClellan, who established his own headquarters in Frederick on September 12, took Lee by surprise. As Longstreet admitted in his memoirs, the "hallucination that McClellan was not capable of serious work seemed to pervade our army, even to this moment of dreadful threatening."[115]

Of course, to say that McClellan's movements upset Lee's plans is a matter of conjecture, given the fact that the Army of Northern Virginia crossed the Potomac without a plan distributed to and understood by its principal commanders. The first detailed plan prepared by Lee was Special Order 191, his response to the crisis as it developed on September 8 and 9, drawn up without input from Longstreet and against the advice of Jackson.

Lastly, Lee assumed that it would be his opponent who would make a misstep of one kind or another and present the Army of Northern Virginia with the chance to win a crushing, if not decisive, battle on Northern soil. In fact, it was Lee who committed the major strategic and operational errors of the campaign and who at Sharpsburg presented McClellan with an opportunity to perhaps win the war in an afternoon.

Nevertheless, given the situation Lee faced after Second Manassas, his decision to retain the initiative and to strike north, while mistaken, is understandable. His expectation that the army would find itself better fed in Maryland than it had been in northern Virginia was not unreasonable. Nor was his supposition that his soldiers, far from deserting the colors, would be eager to remain with an army already flushed with victory and about to cross the mighty Potomac and to visit the horrors of war on the Yankees. And who could have supposed that the first two weeks of September 1862 would mark the high point of George B. McClellan's tenure as commander of the Army of the Potomac? Who would have expected that the Federal regiments, despite their many recent defeats, would fight so well along Antietam Creek?

But if Lee's decision to invade Maryland was defensible, the question nevertheless remains: What lessons did he learn from the experience? Would Lee henceforth eschew hastily planned, similarly half-cocked offensive operations? Would future offensive operations be approved ahead of time by the president, provided with the appropriate available support—manpower and logistical—by the Confederate government, and be well planned and staffed by Lee in cooperation with his principal subordinates? Would Lee continue to overestimate the fighting power of his own army, and to underestimate that of the Army of the Potomac? In short, would Lee recognize the Maryland campaign for the fiasco and near-disaster that it was, and draw the proper conclusions from his experience?

Unfortunately for the Confederacy, Robert E. Lee refused to consider the campaign a failure. As Major Taylor of Lee's staff wrote, the capture of Harpers Ferry "was sufficiently important to compensate for all the trouble experienced."[116] In fact, the commander of the Army of Northern Virginia longed for the opportunity to strike north again and to engage the enemy in battle. He wrote President Davis only four days after Sharpsburg:

> The army is resting to-day on the Opequon, below Martinsburg. Its present efficiency is greatly paralyzed by the loss to its ranks of the numerous stragglers. I have taken every means in my power from the beginning to correct this evil, which has increased instead of diminished. A great many men belonging to the army never entered Maryland at all; many returned after getting there, while others who crossed the river kept aloof. The stream has not lessened since crossing the Potomac, though the cavalry has been constantly employed in

endeavoring to arrest it. . . . It occasions me the greatest concern in the future operations of the army, for it is still my desire to threaten a passage into Maryland, to occupy the enemy on this frontier, and, if my purpose cannot be accomplished, to draw them into the Valley, where I can attack them to advantage.[117]

Taylor noted that Lee "was most anxious to recross into Maryland but was persuaded by his principal advisors that the condition of the army did not warrant such a move. This is conjecture on my part. I only know of his opinion & *guess* why he did not follow it."[118] Lee, despite the pitiful condition of his "poorly clad, barefooted patriots," refused to resign himself to defensive operations. When the opportunity to move north presented itself again, Lee was prepared to strike, and to strike quickly, in much the same fashion as he had in early September 1862.

2

The Gettysburg Campaign

"Our Success at Gettysburg Was Not As Great As Reported"

As LEE'S ARMY RECOVERED ITS STRENGTH in the Shenandoah Valley, in late October and early November of 1862, McClellan led his army back across the Potomac east of the Blue Ridge Mountains and once again shifted the seat of the war within the eastern theater to northern Virginia. To counter McClellan, Lee left Jackson, now commanding the reorganized Army of Northern Virginia's Second Corps, in the Shenandoah Valley, while Longstreet, now in command of the First Corps, marched east to Culpeper Court House to prevent the Federals from moving further south than the upper Rappahannock River.

On November 7, Major General Ambrose E. Burnside took command of the Army of the Potomac under orders from Washington to conduct an offensive toward Richmond. Burnside disliked the idea of an offensive along the Warrenton-Culpeper axis. As the Federals moved south, Jackson's troops in the valley would be perfectly positioned to cut Burnside's line of communications running back along the Orange & Alexandria Railroad. Burnside developed an alternate plan that Lincoln and Halleck reluctantly accepted. The Army of the Potomac would prepare for a direct assault, but instead sidestep to the east, shift its communications to a shorter and more secure route that led back to the Potomac River landing at Aquia Creek, make a surprise crossing of the Rappahannock near Fredericksburg, and begin the march on Richmond.

Unfortunately for the new Union commander, bad weather and late-arriving pontoons precluded a surprise crossing of the river. As Burnside waited for conditions to improve, Lee quickly moved Longstreet's corps into a strong position around Fredericksburg and advised Jackson to prepare to abandon the valley and to march his corps to the east in preparation for battle.

The written and oral communications that passed between Lee and Jackson in November and December 1862 are of particular interest. First, Lee's letters to Jackson well illustrate not only the former's confidence in his most trusted corps commander, but also the very decentralized approach to command and control employed within the Army of Northern Virginia. Second, while Fredericksburg was a purely defensive battle, both Lee and Jackson evidently sought more than a defensive victory.

Despite the fact that Burnside's army was more than twice the strength of Longstreet's corps, Lee faced the impending assault with remarkable equanimity and willingness to trust in Jackson's judgment. Lee did not order Jackson to leave the valley, but instead left the decision to his discretion. In a letter of November 23, Lee laid out the situation as he understood it and concluded: "I do not see at this distance, what military effect can be produced by the continuance of your corps in the Valley."[1] Lee advised that if Jackson reached the same conclusion, he ought to "move east of the Blue Ridge and take such a position as you may find best."[2] In subsequent letters of November 25 and 27, Lee provided additional information and suggestions, but no direct orders concerning Jackson's line or rate of march.

Despite the natural strength of the Fredericksburg position, both Lee and Jackson preferred to fight on more open ground.

While the prospects of repulsing Burnside's assault and driving the Federals back across the Rappahannock were good, there was little likelihood that the Army of Northern Virginia would be able to exploit any advantage gained on the battlefield. The powerful Federal artillery batteries placed on Stafford Heights to support the crossing would also cover any retreat. Jackson disliked the idea of fighting at Fredericksburg, and may have been responsible for shaping Lee's views on the matter. Shortly before the battle Jackson admitted to his brother-in-law, Major General Daniel Harvey Hill: "I am opposed to fighting here. We will whip the enemy but gain no fruits of victory. I have advised the line of the North Anna, but have been overruled."[3] Lee, in a letter to Secretary of War James A. Seddon, admitted after the battle:

> I think it more advantageous to retire to the Annas & give battle than on the banks of the Rappahannock. My design was to have done so in the first instance. My purpose was changed not from any advantage in this position, but from an unwillingness to open more of our country to depredation than possible, & also with a view of collecting such forage & provisions as could be obtained in the Rappahannock Valley.[4]

Between December 10 and 12, 1862, Burnside established his bridgeheads across the Rappahannock, and on the thirteenth the Army of the Potomac launched its grand assault. By day's end the Federals had gained little ground and had suffered over ten thousand casualties, twice Lee's losses. The two armies remained in place the next day, collecting their wounded and their dead, both commanders hoping that the other might attack. On the night of December 14 and 15, the Army of the Potomac withdrew across the Rappahannock without interference from Lee's troops. While the Federals continued to threaten and to feint for weeks after their defeat, Fredericksburg brought to an effective end the campaigning season in northern Virginia.

FOR LEE, Fredericksburg epitomized his experience of command during 1862. The battle had been a notable victory, the most easily won of his many triumphs. Nevertheless, Lee remained frustrated and dissatisfied. Since taking over command of the Army of Northern Virginia, Lee had sought not just battlefield success, but the destruction of the Federal armies arrayed against him. Unfortunately, despite his many victories, and the thousands of Confederate casualties suffered, a truly decisive success had thus far eluded him. He wrote his wife on December 16: "This morning [the Federals] were all safe on the north side of the Rappahannock. They went as they came, in the night. They suffered heavily as far as the battle went, but it did not go far enough to satisfy me."[5]

Given his experience of command, Lee might well have concluded that his failure to destroy the armies arrayed against him was rooted in the impracticability of the tactical offensive, especially for an army consistently outnumbered and with a limited supply of manpower. Lee, in fact, did entertain such thoughts, if only briefly. He wrote his wife on Christmas Day that he would have attacked before the Federals withdrew had he known that Burnside had decided not to resume his assault. Nevertheless, Lee admitted, he was "content," for he realized that "we would have gained more but we would have lost more, & perhaps our relative condition would not have been improved. My heart bleeds at the death of every one of our gallant men."[6] But as the Christmas season passed, so, too, did Lee's doubts about his aggressive tactics. In a January 10 letter to Seddon, Lee noted:

> More than once have most promising opportunities been lost for want of men to take advantage of them, and victory itself has been made to put on the appearance of defeat, because our diminished and exhausted troops have been unable to renew a successful struggle against fresh numbers of the enemy.

Nevertheless, the commander of the Army of Northern Virginia had no intention of adopting a less aggressive strategy. He advised Seddon to summon the Southern people to greater efforts and sacrifice. "They must put forth their full strength at once," he wrote.[7]

Lee and Jackson remained committed to an offensive strategy in the eastern theater. On February 23, Jackson directed Jed Hotchkiss "to prepare a map of the Valley of Va. extended to Harrisburg, Pa., and then on to Philadelphia;—wishing the preparation to be kept a profound secret."[8] But despite these preliminary preparations, Lee recognized that a Northern invasion would have to wait until several factors were resolved. First, nothing was possible until the spring, when the ground would be dry and the first crops would be ready for harvest in the fields of Maryland and Pennsylvania. Second, he recognized the possibility, if not the probability, that the better supplied and manned Army of the Potomac would break its camps first and attempt yet another move toward the south. Third, Lee needed to reconcentrate his own army, which, during the course of the winter, had lost several formations to the garrison of Richmond, coastal North Carolina, and southeastern Virginia. Fourth, Lee wanted his army reinforced and supplied to the greatest extent possible to lessen the odds against him. Fifth, and perhaps most important, Lee needed to convince President Davis and the government to support wholeheartedly plans for an offensive in the East.

Complicating this whole equation was the deteriorating Confederate position in the western theater of operations. After Kirby Smith's victory at Richmond in August 1862, the tide of war in the West had turned against the Confederacy. The South lost the battles of Corinth (October 3–4) and Murfreesboro (December 31, 1862–January 3, 1863). In late December, Federal forces reached Vicksburg, Mississippi. While the initial Union assault against the city failed, by late January 1863 Major General Ulysses S. Grant had moved his entire army to Vicksburg and threatened to cut the Confederacy in two.

In the late winter and early spring of 1863, President Jefferson Davis and Secretary of War James A. Seddon searched for some method that would allow them to reverse the course of the war in the West and to repulse the expected Federal attacks in the Carolinas without undermining the position of the only army—Lee's—that had yet to yield ground to the Federals. The answer to the strategic problem facing the Confederacy was by no measure a simple one, nor were the two men most responsible for finding a solution of one mind with regard to the future course of the war.

Davis was the more knowledgeable and experienced of the two in military affairs. The fifty-five-year-old Kentucky-born Confederate president was an 1828 graduate of West Point and, as was the case with many of his generals, a veteran of the Mexican War. But the ill health that so often plagued Davis's presidency ensured an early end to his military career. He resigned in 1835, although he returned to the army to serve in the Mexican War. His poor health, compounded by a wound suffered at the battle of Buena Vista, led him to bid farewell to the military a second time in 1847. National politics became Davis's new forum, and the now prominent Mississippi planter represented his state in the U.S. Senate from 1847 to 1851, then served as secretary of war in the cabinet of President Franklin Pierce from 1853 to 1857. Davis returned to the Senate in the latter year, where he became an outspoken advocate of states' rights, though an opponent of secession. But when Mississippi left the Union, Davis resigned from the Senate and in February 1861 became the provisional—and a year later the elected—president of the Confederacy.

Seddon was a forty-seven-year-old graduate of the University of Virginia with no military experience. A trained lawyer, he had been active in state politics before the war and had served briefly in the U.S. Congress. He was considered by many to be a gifted speaker with a fine mind, but his executive skills were limited and his weak health a constant handicap to all that he undertook.

After being named as secretary of war in late November 1862, Seddon, despite the near total absence of martial seasoning, quickly identified the West as the Confederacy's Achilles' heel. He attempted to shape a coherent national policy for the theater, but, as had often been the case in his life, his lack of executive and political acumen offset the power of his ideas.[9]

Davis and Seddon knew that their armies in the West were almost always outnumbered and all too often outgeneraled as well. One solution would be to find another commander as capable as Robert E. Lee, someone who could fight outnumbered and win. But none of the South's senior generals were as able as the commander of the Army of Northern Virginia, nor was Davis at that point in the war willing to replace one of the more senior generals, such as Lieutenant General Braxton Bragg (Davis's favorite) or Joseph E. Johnston (Seddon's favorite), with a more junior, but perhaps more competent, officer. That being the case, the most obvious alternative was to find reinforcements for the armies in the West, and to a lesser degree the Carolinas. Unfortunately, the Confederacy had few reserves, and if reinforcements were to be sent west or south, Seddon concluded that they would have to be stripped from the forces deployed in the eastern theater, most likely from Lee's Army of Northern Virginia. By late March, Seddon had begun to consider the possibility of drawing forces from the East. Such a move made strategic sense: using the Confederacy's interior lines to switch forces from one theater to the other; applying on a national scale the movements Lee had profitably employed within his theater when he switched his own forces between the Shenandoah Valley and eastern Virginia.

On April 1, Seddon first raised the issue, not with Lee, but with Major General Samuel Jones, the commander of the Confederate forces in western Virginia. Seddon advised Jones:

> It is possible even that a brigade or a regiment or two may be called for to join a force to be sent from here to the reenforcement of General Bragg's army. The President has such a step under consideration, and if advices from Hooker's army render it likely he will not advance, it is not unlikely the thought may ripen into action.[10]

On April 6, Seddon advised Lee of the possibility of a transfer, noting that some Federal troops from the Army of the Potomac had already gone west. Seddon wrote:

> It is, of course, very important to re-enforce General Bragg's army; but the Department, after anxiously surveying all the resources at command, is unable to find troops at its disposal for that end, unless they can safely be sent from the forces in this department. If two or three brigades, say of Pickett's division, to be united with another that may be possibly made up from General Samuel Jones' command, could be spared, they would be an encouraging re-enforcement to the Army of the West.
>
> It would seem natural that when so large a portion of the troops meant to be guarded against here, as Burnside's division from Newport News, have been withdrawn to the west, they should be met there by a withdrawal of at least a part of our defensive reserves here. I know, however, that your army is largely outnumbered by the enemy in your front, and that it is not unlikely that a movement against you may be made at an early day. I am, therefore, unwilling to send beyond your command any portion even of the forces here without your counsel and approval. I should ask, therefore, your consideration of the subject and the result of your reflections at your earliest convenience.[11]

Lee, not surprisingly, had little interest in seeing any of his troops sent west. He knew that the Army of the Potomac, now commanded by Major General Joseph Hooker, was preparing for yet another campaign in northern Virginia. Lee, with his own much smaller army scattered about eastern Virginia, was hardly in a position to surrender troops, at least not until the expected Federal attack had been repulsed. Nevertheless, Lee, who was not only the commander of the Army of Northern Virginia but also Davis's principal military adviser, had to admit that the bleak situation in the West demanded action of some kind. Lee wrote Seddon on April 9:

The most natural way to re-enforce General Johnston would seem to be to transfer a portion of the troops from this department to oppose those sent west, but it is not so easy for us to change troops from one department to another as it is for the enemy, and if we rely upon that method we may be always too late.

Should General Hooker's army assume the defensive, the readiest method of relieving the pressure upon General Johnston and General Beauregard [at Charleston] would be for this army to cross into Maryland. This cannot be done, however, in the present condition of the roads, nor unless I can obtain a certain amount of provisions and suitable transportation. But this is what I would recommend, if practicable.[12]

Lee's unwillingness to offer any of his troops for transfer was both understandable and, given the situation in early April, perfectly sensible. As events would show, Lee was heavily outnumbered when Hooker's army crossed the Rappahannock in late April 1863. But Lee's recommendation that an offensive in the East was the best way to reverse the course of the war in the West was a bold, and also a strategically questionable, assumption.

Despite Lee's negative response, the pressure from Richmond to detach troops continued. On April 14, Samuel Cooper, the adjutant and inspector general of the army, wrote Lee on Davis's behalf. Could Lee not "spare Hood's or Picket's division" to reinforce Tennessee?[13] Lee replied on the sixteenth, noting that Hooker's large army would not long remain quiescent and that the Army of Northern Virginia was already dangerously understrength. Lee also downplayed the threat to Vicksburg, suggesting that the summer season would force an end to Grant's operations. Lee then reiterated his recommendation for an invasion.

I think it all-important that we should assume the aggressive by the 1st of May, when we may expect General Hooker's army to be weakened by the expiration of the term of service of many of his regiments, and before new recruits can be received. If we could be placed in a condition to make a vigorous advance at that time, I think the Valley could be swept of [Brigadier General Robert H.] Milroy, and the army opposite me be thrown north of the Potomac. I believe greater relief would in this way be afforded to the armies in Middle Tennessee and on the Carolina coast than by any other method.

Nevertheless, Lee quite rightly pointed out that the ultimate responsibility for the decision rested with the president. "I recommend," Lee wrote, "that he follow the dictates of his good judgment."[14]

Having parried the requests for troops, at least for the time being, Lee set about pressuring the authorities in Richmond for reinforcements and supplies for his own army and to hasten to it his detached units.[15] Far from yielding troops to meet the threat in the West, Lee was actually strengthening his army. The immediate threat from Hooker was sufficient to account for Lee's actions, although he also had his mind set on his proposed Northern offensive.

While the issue of future troop transfers to the West remained unresolved in Richmond, before Davis, Seddon, or Cooper could further pressure Lee, the Federal Army of the Potomac opened its spring offensive and made the point moot. On April 27, Hooker began his right hook around Lee's left flank—the first move of the Chancellorsville campaign. By the twenty-ninth, several Federal corps were well positioned in Lee's rear, but Hooker dallied and failed to make the most of his early advantage. Lee was able to fend off the forces on his flank as well as those threatening a direct assault across the Rappahannock at Fredericksburg. Hooker unwisely halted and dug in, surrendering the initiative to Lee, who on the morning of May 2 sent Jackson on a daring flank march into Hooker's rear. At dusk, Jackson attacked, striking and rolling up the flank of the Federal Eleventh Corps. Unfortunately for Lee, amidst the confusion, Confederate skirmishers shot Jackson, shattering his arm.[16] Under the cover of darkness, the Federal commanders recovered from Jackson's blow and stabilized the Union line. The Rebels, in an attempt to make the most of their advantage, pressed the attack, driving back Hooker's army. But with the Army of the Potomac's flanks resting securely on the river, it would not budge. When Lee's assaults ended, Hooker, against the counsel of many of his corps commanders, chose to withdraw. Early on the morning of May 6, the Federals recrossed the river.

For Lee, Chancellorsville had been a brilliant victory, although the costs of the battle were high. Federal losses were 17,287 in an army of 110,000; those of the Confederates, 12,764 in an army of 43,000.[17] Lee had also lost Stonewall Jackson, the army's most gifted corps commander and Lee's principal adviser and confidant.

AS THE FEDERAL TROOPS WITHDREW, Lee's mind once again turned to the possibility of an offensive. He knew that there was no time to waste, for he could expect renewed demands for troops now that he had thrown back Hooker's army. On May 7, Lee wrote a long, preemptive letter to President Davis, bemoaning the fact that in the last battle the army had been outnumbered almost three to one:

> I bring these facts to Your Excellency's notice now that you may take such means as in your judgment seem best to increase the strength of the army. This can be done, in my opinion, by bringing troops from the departments of South Carolina, Georgia, and Florida. No more can be needed there this summer than enough to maintain the water batteries. Nor do I think that more will be required at Wilmington than are sufficient for this purpose. If they are kept in their present positions in these departments, they will perish of disease. I know there will be difficulties raised to their withdrawal. But it will be better to order General Beauregard in with all the forces which can be spared, and to put him in command here, than to keep them there inactive and this army inefficient from paucity of numbers.

There are many things about which I would like to
consult Your Excellency, and I should be delighted, if your
health and convenience suited, if you could visit the army. I
could get you a comfortable room in the vicinity of my headquarters, and I know you would be content with our camp
fare. Should this, however, be inconvenient, I will endeavor
to go to Richmond, though I feel my presence here now is
essential.[18]

Lee, who on previous occasions had taken great pains to
keep his commander in chief away from headquarters, now
wished to meet with Davis in the field, rather than in the capital. In Richmond, the Confederate president would be sur-
rounded by advisers, such as Seddon, who seemed intent not on
reinforcing the Army of Northern Virginia, but on detaching
from it troops for service in the West. If Davis could be enticed
to visit the army's headquarters, Lee would be able to convince
an isolated president of the wisdom of an offensive campaign in
northern Virginia.

As Lee suspected, the secretary of war had not yet given up
on his scheme to transfer troops to the West. On May 9, Seddon sent a telegraph to Lee suggesting the possibility of sending George Pickett's division to Mississippi. Because of alleged
trouble deciphering the message, Lee did not reply until the
tenth. In a short telegram and longer letter, he advised the secretary of war that the "distance and the uncertainty of the em-
ployment of the troops" was "unfavorable" (though the same
was not apparently true with regard to Lee's request that Seddon move troops from Florida to reinforce Lee's army). Lee also
reiterated his conviction that "the climate in June will force the
enemy to retire" from Vicksburg. Moreover, Lee threatened
Seddon, warning that if the Army of Northern Virginia was not
reinforced, its commander might feel "obliged to withdraw into
the defenses around Richmond."[19] Nevertheless, Lee informed
the secretary of war that if he considered the transfer necessary,
he ought to "order Pickett at once."[20] In short, if the troops
were to go west, Seddon would have to order the movement

over Lee's objection, and risk the political fallout that would come if Lee moved the Army of Northern Virginia closer to the capital. If the secretary of war was, in fact, prepared to take such a step, his hands were tied, for when Davis read Lee's reply, he noted that the answer "was such as I should have anticipated, and in which I concur."[21]

The next day, Lee sent another letter to Richmond, this one addressed to the president, suggesting the propriety of an offensive in the East.[22] The commander of the Army of Northern Virginia then followed up his communication by hastening to the Confederate capital.[23]

Lee, accompanied by Jeb Stuart, arrived in the capital on May 14, along with depressing news from the West—the Confederate forces had suffered another setback, this time near Jackson, Mississippi.[24] J. B. Jones, a clerk in the War Department, wrote in his diary that there was "a dark cloud over the hopes of patriots, for Vicksburg is seriously endangered. Its fall would be the worst blow we have yet received." The next day, Jones noted that Lee was "long closeted" with Davis and Seddon. At this meeting, the president decided that Pickett would rejoin Lee's army, and not move west.[25]

On Saturday, May 16, Lee met with Davis and his cabinet in what most historians portray as a debate over Lee's proposed strategy for an offensive in the East. While there was certainly a great deal of discussion, there was actually very little debate. The fact that Pickett that very morning was marching his troops, accompanied by two regiments of North Carolina cavalry, through the city on their way north, indicates that Davis and Seddon had already cast their die and decided to adopt Lee's plans. Davis's decision to involve his full cabinet in the decision-making process was more of a formality, a search for support, and, perhaps, also an attempt to spread the responsibility for what he knew to be a high-stakes gamble.

In the cabinet meeting, Lee laid out the rationale for his offensive, basically restating those points he had been making in his letters to Davis, Seddon, and Cooper since early April 1863.

A march north across the Potomac would forestall a renewed Federal offensive against Richmond, allow Lee to feed his army on Northern soil, and force the Federals to shift troops from the West to the East. The only member of the cabinet to oppose Lee was John H. Reagan, the postmaster general.[26] As a Texan, Reagan was deeply concerned about the ever-worsening course of the war in the West. He considered, as he later wrote, "the importance and necessity of holding Vicksburg and Port Hudson, and thereby preserving our communications with the States west of the Mississippi" as "a matter of serious consequence." But the opinions, and fears, of the postmaster general were not about to sway Davis from his continued faith in the advice of the Confederacy's most successful general.

After a grueling, daylong discussion, the cabinet agreed with Davis to support Lee's proposal for an offensive across the Potomac River, a move that would threaten Washington, Baltimore, and Philadelphia. Unfortunately, Reagan's memoir, the only account of the meeting—but one written more than thirty years after the event—made no mention of several important aspects of Lee's plan addressed in previous correspondence. Had he asked the cabinet to move Beauregard and units from the Carolinas to northern Virginia? Had Lee provided Davis, Seddon, or the cabinet with anything approaching a detailed plan of operations, or a timetable for the forthcoming invasion? According to Reagan's account, the answer to these questions was no. Lee portrayed his Northern march as a supply-gathering expedition that would also threaten Northern cities and disrupt Federal plans in both the eastern and western theaters. Did Lee mention the prospects of fighting a major battle north of the Potomac? Apparently not, although Reagan suspected that Lee "favored such a campaign because he believed he commanded an invincible army, which had been victorious in so many battles, and in all of them against greatly preponderating numbers and resources."[27] While Reagan's failure to mention or to elucidate these points might be dismissed as evidence of declining mental faculties, the correspondence that passed between Lee and Davis over the next few weeks supports the contention that the Confederate president and his cabinet possessed an incomplete understanding of what Lee actually had in mind for the campaign.

LEE RETURNED TO HIS HEADQUARTERS in Fredericksburg with his mind set on his planned offensive across the Potomac. Nevertheless, he knew that the context within which Davis had approved the proposal could change. After all, with regard to the course of operations in the western theater, Lee had offered his scheme for an invasion of the North as more of a long-term, rather than an immediate, solution to the deteriorating situation in the West. For the present, to save Vicksburg Lee expected Pemberton to resist, Johnston to harass, and the summer season ultimately to force Grant to retire. But what if Pemberton faltered, Johnston failed to move, Grant persisted, and the loss of Vicksburg appeared imminent?

Lee, having won his "battle of Richmond," now found himself in a difficult position. He had to launch his offensive as soon as possible, for if he delayed and the Federals threatened to capture Vicksburg, there would be renewed demands made on Davis to detach troops from the Army of Northern Virginia for service in the West. Moreover, once Lee's grand offensive was under way, he would have to fight and to win a major battle, preferably on the north bank of the Potomac, for he had assured the cabinet that a Northern invasion would redress the imbalance of forces in the West. A victorious battle was the only certain way to secure that end.

But how was Lee to prepare his army in such a short time for such a demanding operation? At Chancellorsville, the Army of Northern Virginia, while triumphant, had suffered 25 to 30 percent casualties. These men had to be replaced. Lee had to reconcentrate, bringing Longstreet and his divisions north to the Rappahannock. Lee also needed additional reinforcements to strengthen his army, especially in the cavalry arm, and sought the formation of a second mini-army, or corps of observation, under Beauregard, in northern Virginia.

Amidst these efforts, Lee, now without Jackson's services, believed he had to reorganize the army from a two corps to a three corps structure, with accompanying alterations in the organization of the cavalry, artillery, and staffs. When the army marched north, less than three weeks after Lee's return from Richmond, two of the three men leading corps and three of the nine men leading divisions were untested at their new levels of command. New brigadiers commanded seven, and colonels another six, of Lee's thirty-seven brigades.[28] As Douglas Southall Freeman wrote:

> To explain this reorganization is largely to explain Gettysburg. Nothing happened on that field that could not be read in the roster of the army, the peculiarities and inexperience of the new leaders, the distribution of the units, and the inevitable confusion of a staff that had to be enlarged or extemporized to direct troops with which it was unacquainted.[29]

Such dramatic changes in the organization and leadership of the Army of Northern Virginia suggested the need for delay, not haste. But Lee, having oversold the benefits of his scheme for a Northern invasion, and anxious to avoid future demands upon him to detach troops for service in the West, was compelled by circumstances of his own making to embark on an undertaking of incalculable importance with the largest, but in some ways the most fragile, army he had yet commanded.

Lee's fears that Davis might yet reverse himself and direct the transfer of troops from Virginia to the West were well founded. As disappointing news from the West continued to reach the capital, Davis, who had been ill much of the winter and early spring, suffered a relapse. On May 19, the clerk Jones noted that the president was "too ill" to come to his office and that there was talk that he was in a perhaps fatal "decline."[30] On the twenty-sixth, Davis, under renewed pressure to find reinforcements for the West, and plagued by doubts about his decision, called another "all day" cabinet meeting, but when only Reagan spoke out against Lee's plan, Davis remained committed to a Northern invasion.[31]

There was no such vacillation in Fredericksburg, where Lee labored to prepare his army for the advance. Despite herculean efforts, the commander of the Army of Northern Virginia achieved only mixed results. After all, the units that were to reinforce Lee's army had to come from other forces commanded by generals who, like Lee, were not enthusiastic about surrendering men. The most notable was Daniel Harvey Hill, commanding in North Carolina, who was unwilling to detach his own troops for service in northern Virginia without a direct command.[32] When Hill failed to respond to the commander of the Army of Northern Virginia's repeated advices and "discretionary orders," Lee, his mind focused on the forthcoming campaign, grew frustrated. On May 30, he dictated two harsh and somewhat disingenuous letters—one for Davis and the other for Seddon—requesting that he be relieved of his responsibility for overseeing the department of North Carolina, complaining of Hill's lack of cooperation, and stressing the need for a concentration of force. Lee warned the president, "I feel the time has passed when I could have taken the offensive with advantage"; while in the letter to the secretary of war, he impressed upon Seddon the wisdom of transferring troops to the Army of Northern Virginia from the coastal regions of the Carolinas.[33] But all Harvey Hill had done when pressed for troops was to respond in the same fashion as had Lee: doubting the wisdom of such transfers and refusing to part with irreplaceable units without a direct order. As for the implication that Hill's reluctance to yield troops might have jeopardized the invasion plan, this accusation, while no doubt meant to spur Davis to take action, was grossly unfair and inaccurate. It was the reorganization of the army, and not Hill's recalcitrance, that delayed the advance.

Lee's letter prompted a long and equally curious reply from the president. Davis wrote that he

> had never fairly comprehended your views and purposes un-
> til the receipt of your letter of yesterday, and now have to re-
> gret that I did not earlier know all that you had communicated
> to others. I could hardly have misunderstood you, and need
> not say would have been glad to second your wishes, confid-
> ing, as I always do, as well in your judgment as in your infor-
> mation.[34]

As Edwin Coddington wrote in his study of the Gettysburg campaign, the correspondence that passed between Davis and Lee
"makes one wonder what in fact the two men did discuss during Lee's several visits to Richmond."[35]

Davis's letter also revealed that he was deeply concerned,
not just about the course of the war in the West, but also about
the prospects for victory in the East, and especially the security
of Richmond. The president wanted Lee to retain responsibility for the Carolina coast, although he wished that he knew

> how to relieve you from all anxiety concerning movements on
> the York or James River against Richmond while you are mov-
> ing toward the north and west; but even if you could spare
> troops for the purpose, on whom could you devolve the com-
> mand with that feeling of security which would be necessary
> for the full execution of your designs?

Davis, obviously wracked by doubts, concluded: "It is useless
to look back, and it would be unkind to annoy you in the midst
of your many cares with the reflections which I have not been
able to avoid."[36]

Lee responded on June 2, calling for additional reinforcements, but assuring the worried Davis that "if I am able to
move, I propose to do so cautiously, watching the result, and not
to get beyond recall until I find it safe." He also advised the
president that Grant's reported movement toward the Yazoo River
might well be "for the purpose of reaching their transports and
retiring from the contest,"[37] the very course that Lee had earlier predicted would happen with the approach of summer.

THE VERY NEXT DAY, JUNE 3, the Army of Northern Virginia began its march toward the Shenandoah Valley. While Stuart's cavalry screened the movement, Stonewall Jackson's old Second Corps, now commanded by Lieutenant General Richard Stoddert Ewell, led the advance west, followed by Longstreet's First Corps. The newly established Third Corps, commanded by Lieutenant General A. P. Hill, guarded the Rappahannock crossing at Fredericksburg, opposite the Army of the Potomac.

Despite the significance of the undertaking, Lee's letters to Davis and Seddon made no mention that the initial phase of the invasion had begun. In a June 7 letter to Davis, Lee portrayed the westward march as a maneuver to counter Federal movements.[38] The next day, Lee informed the secretary of war:

> As far as I can judge, there is nothing to be gained by this army remaining quietly on the defensive, which it must do unless it can be re-enforced. I am aware that there is difficulty and hazard in taking the aggressive with so large an army in its front, intrenched behind a river, where it cannot be advantageously attacked. Unless it can be drawn out in a position to be assailed, it will take its own time to prepare and strengthen itself to renew its advance upon Richmond, and force this army back within the intrenchments of that city. This may be the result in any event; still, I think it is worth a trial to prevent such a catastrophe. Still, if the Department thinks it better to remain on the defensive, and guard as far as possible all the avenues of approach, and await the time of the enemy, I am ready to adopt this course. You have, therefore, only to inform me.[39]

On the ninth, in a letter to Davis written from Culpeper, Lee acknowledged that his cavalry had been engaged at Brandy Station, but once again implied that his movements were defensive in nature, designed to forestall a Federal attack.[40]

Nevertheless, as Lee's reports reached Richmond, Davis, Seddon, and even the War Department clerks assumed that the movements of the Army of Northern Virginia were not defensive, but offensive in nature.[41] But Davis never did receive an "official" confirmation of the start of the invasion from Lee. In a June 15 letter, written the very day that the army began to cross into Maryland, Lee outlined Ewell's successful operations in the Shenandoah Valley and his advance "toward the Potomac" but made no mention of any crossing of the river. Lee portrayed himself as someone uncommitted to such a course and warned Davis that

> the uncertainty of the reports as to threatened expeditions of the enemy along the coast of North Carolina and between the Rappahannock and James rivers in Virginia, has caused delay in the movements of this army, and it may now be too late to accomplish all that was desired.[42]

On June 23, only a week before the battle of Gettysburg, Lee once again raised the question of a command in northern Virginia for Beauregard. Such a force, Lee advised Davis, would shield Richmond and, more importantly, provide a diversion south of the river that might lead the Federals to divide their forces, at least by implication suggesting that Lee already had taken, or intended to take, the Army of Northern Virginia over to the north bank. But, Lee wrote: "If success should attend the operations of this army, and what I now suggest would greatly increase the probability of that reality, we might even hope to compel the recall of some of the enemy's troops from the west."[43] Lee, who had several times in his dispatches and in person assured Davis, Seddon, Cooper, and the cabinet that an offensive across the Potomac would force the Federals to transfer troops from the West, now spoke only of "hope," and not assurance. Moreover, Lee now linked a favorable outcome to the concentration of a corps under Beauregard in northern Virginia, a suggestion that Lee had made several times in the past, but had never posed as a sine qua non to his plan.

Lee's June 23 letter is an interesting, and in some ways puzzling, document. Why, at this late date, was he still unwilling to inform Davis that the Army of Northern Virginia had crossed the Potomac? A desire for secrecy suggests a ready answer, for dispatches—as the events of the 1862 Maryland campaign had demonstrated—could fall into enemy hands. Certainly, it would have been foolish for Lee to detail his plan of operations in a dispatch sent back to Richmond. But why refrain from even mentioning that the army had already passed the river? Is it possible that more than a week after Ewell had entered Maryland, and days after his van had crossed into Pennsylvania, Lee believed that the presence of twenty thousand Rebel troops north of the Potomac had somehow gone unnoticed by the Federals? Rather, the similarities in tone evident in Lee's letters to Davis at the start of the Gettysburg *and* the Maryland campaigns suggests that the principal aim of the commander of the Army of Northern Virginia was not secrecy, but obfuscation. Moreover, what is the historian to make of Lee's call for Davis to bring Beauregard to Culpeper at what, in retrospect, appears to be late in the day—only a week before the battle of Gettysburg? Even if Davis, who had thus far ignored Lee's earlier suggestions, took prompt action, at least a fortnight would pass before Beauregard could concentrate even a small force in northern Virginia. Assuming that Lee's recommendation was made in good faith, and not simply in an attempt to provide an excuse should the invasion fail, this proposed course of action indicates that Lee considered the campaign still in an early phase, with weeks, if not months, of marching to come. As he had the previous summer when the army entered Maryland, Lee assumed that he would be able to roam about the Northern countryside for quite some time before being challenged by the slow reacting, and laggardly moving, Army of the Potomac. According to William Allan, Lee "expected therefore to move about, to maneuver & alarm the enemy, threaten their cities, hit any blows he might be able to do without risking a general battle, & then towards fall return nearer his base."[44]

Lee followed up his June 23 letter with an even more remarkable dispatch penned two days later. The commander of the Army of Northern Virginia declared himself incommunicado (he would not write Davis again until July 4, after the battle of Gettysburg) and further lowered the president's expectations for a successful campaign. "I have not sufficient troops to maintain my communications," Lee wrote, "and, therefore, have to abandon them. I think I can throw General Hooker's army across the Potomac and draw troops from the south, embarrassing their plan of campaign in a measure, if I can do nothing more and have to return."[45] Poor Jefferson Davis! After supporting Lee's plans for an invasion of the North, despite incredible political pressure and the inclinations of the secretary of war to send some of Lee's troops west to save Vicksburg, the Confederate president must have been shocked to learn that the commander of the Army of Northern Virginia, in the midst of his invasion, was now prepared to guarantee nothing more than the hope that he might upset and embarrass Federal plans "in a measure."

IF THE EXTANT DOCUMENTATION regarding Lee's intentions and campaign objectives in the spring and early summer of 1863 is incomplete and contradictory, his post-campaign correspondence provides even fewer insights into the workings of his mind. In his initial report, dated July 31, 1863, Lee wrote that the

> position occupied by the enemy opposite Fredericksburg being one in which he could not be attacked to advantage, it was determined to draw him from it. The execution of this purpose embraced the relief of the Shenandoah Valley from the troops that had occupied the lower part of it during the winter and spring, and, if practicable, the transfer of the scene of hostilities north of the Potomac. It was thought that the corresponding movements on the part of the enemy to which those contemplated by us would probably give rise, might offer a fair opportunity to strike a blow at the army then commanded by General Hooker, and that in any event that army would be compelled to leave Virginia, and, possibly, to draw to its support troops designed to operate against other parts of the country. In this way it was supposed that the enemy's plan

of campaign for the summer would be broken up, and part of the season of active operations be consumed in the formation of new combinations, and the preparations that they would require. In addition to these advantages, it was hoped that other valuable results might be attained by military success.[46]

A sympathetic reader could infer from some of the phrases quoted above—for example, Lee's assertion that his maneuvers would "draw to [the Army of the Potomac's] support troops designed to operate against other parts of the country"—that he was there referring to the assurances he had offered the government in April and May that an invasion of Pennsylvania would bring about a realignment of forces in the West. Lee's inability to state that fact forthrightly suggests that he was attempting to lessen the significance of his defeat. Lee was even more circumspect in his formal, and otherwise much more detailed, report on the campaign prepared in January 1864. Gone were the inferences to the expected impact of the eastern offensive on the situation in the West. Nor was there any mention of battle, of Lee's hope that he might discover "a fair opportunity to strike a blow at the army then commanded by General Hooker." Instead, Lee wrote:

Upon the retreat of the Federal Army, commanded by Major-General Hooker, from Chancellorsville, it reoccupied the ground north of the Rappahannock, opposite Fredericksburg, where it could not be attacked excepting at a disadvantage. It was determined to draw it from this position, and, if practicable, to transfer the scene of hostilities beyond the Potomac. The execution of this purpose also embraced the expulsion of the force under General Milroy, which had infested the lower Shenandoah Valley during the preceding winter and spring. If unable to attain the valuable results which might be expected to follow a decided advantage gained over the enemy in Maryland or Pennsylvania, it was hoped that we should at least so far disturb his plan for the summer campaign as to prevent its execution during the season of active operations.[47]

If one considers the above an accurate inventory of Lee's objectives, the Gettysburg campaign must be considered a marked Confederate success! After all, Lee did end the Federal infestation of the valley and did disrupt the Federal plans for a summer campaign in the East.[48]

Lee's reports, especially that of January 1864, have permitted historians to downplay the significance of his failure in the Gettysburg campaign. For example, Douglas Southall Freeman discusses fully Lee's April 1863 assertions that an offensive across the Potomac was "the readiest method of relieving pressure upon General Johnston and General Beauregard . . ." in the second volume of his biography.[49] But 150 pages later, in the third volume, Freeman's discussion of Lee's objectives for the Gettysburg campaign makes no mention of the supposed benefits for the West.[50] The two often-conflicting reports also obscure the importance of battle in Lee's scheme of campaign. After the war, Lee's few remarks remained consistent with the tone of his final January 1864 report. During an 1868 conversation with William Allan, Lee remarked that he "did not want to fight, unless he could get a good opportunity to hit them in detail." Nevertheless, Allan noted, Lee expected to have to give battle at some point "before his return in the Fall."[51]

Many historians have chosen to take Lee's January 1864 report and postwar statements at face value. In *Why the South Lost the Civil War,* Richard E. Beringer, Herman Hattaway, Archer Jones, and William N. Still Jr. termed the Gettysburg campaign "a raid."[52] In their view Lee, while he was prepared to fight a battle on ground and under conditions of his own choosing, did not seek battle per se. His principal objectives were to subsist his army north of the Potomac and to upset Federal plans for the summer. Nevertheless, other historians, most recently Emory Thomas, have written that battle was central to Lee's plans. Thomas concluded: "Regardless of what Lee said or wrote to Davis, what Lee did make clear was his desire to fight a climactic battle on Northern soil. He still sought a showdown, a battle of annihilation that would end the war in a single afternoon."[53]

The memoirs of two of Lee's wartime aides support the view that Lee, as he had himself admitted in his July 31 report, hoped to fight a battle. Colonel A. L. Long, Lee's military secretary, suggested that battle held a prominent position in Lee's plan and that a major victory won on the north bank of the Potomac "would very likely cause the fall of Washington city and the flight of the Federal Government" as well as a diversion of troops from the West.[54] Charles Marshall, then a major, and who in 1863 was Lee's aide-de-camp, actually drafted Lee's January 1864 report on the Gettysburg campaign.[55] Nevertheless, Marshall wrote in his memoir that "General Lee was not unmindful of the valuable results that might follow a decided success in the field."[56] Lee understood that a major victory won on Northern soil would have far greater impact than a comparable victory attained south of the Potomac. Marshall also wrote that Lee believed that a marked battlefield victory could possibly bring an end to the war or, at the least, the withdrawal of Federal troops from the western theater.[57] "Indeed," Marshall noted, "it was in the hope and expectation that his movement northwards, if attended by any considerable military success, would relieve the pressure of the enemy in the South West, that General Lee began his campaign."[58]

While the historical record might well be taken to support the view that Lee did seek battle, the documentary record is sufficiently unclear to permit differing interpretations. Only the enigmatic Lee knew for sure, and it was not his wont to share his intentions fully with anyone. In all probability, no formal plan of campaign has ever surfaced because none ever existed. After all, Lee invaded Maryland in 1862 without a formal plan of campaign, and he would launch his October 1863 Bristoe Station offensive without one, too. All that the historian can say with absolute certainty is that Robert E. Lee sought and gained approval from Jefferson Davis for an invasion of the North by the Army of Northern Virginia that was expected both to safeguard Richmond *and* to bring about a redress in the imbalance of forces in the western theater. Lee planned to move his army west from the vicinity of Fredericksburg, through Culpeper, and thence into the Shenandoah Valley. He intended at that point to move down the valley, clearing it of Federal forces. Assuming his army had not met some unforeseen setback, Lee then expected to cross the Potomac, perhaps with a corps, or perhaps with the entire army, pass through western Maryland, and enter central Pennsylvania. The Gettysburg campaign was, in its details, a campaign of improvisation, with Lee determining his future course of action from the saddle. Questions involving the timing of the crossing and the strength of the forces sent over to the north bank of the Potomac were settled only as the campaign unfolded.[59] No doubt Lee set out from his headquarters at Fredericksburg with myriad possibilities already considered and resolved in his own mind, but he shared few, if any, of his thoughts with his staff, his principal subordinates—Longstreet, Ewell, and Hill—or even the president of the Confederacy.

While Lee, a man of marked military genius, possessed the intellectual talents to organize and to command a vast campaign in such a fashion, there were nevertheless a variety of pitfalls inherent in his fairly secretive, personally compartmentalized, and ad hoc approach to an offensive operation. If Lee possessed a clearly defined objective for the campaign, he never communicated that goal to anyone (or perhaps it would be more accurate to say that he communicated different objectives, to different people, at different times). Military historians consider a clearly defined objective one of the almost universally accepted principles of war. But what was Lee's objective? Was it to seek out and defeat the Army of the Potomac? Was it to threaten Baltimore, Philadelphia, and Washington? Was it to gather supplies for the army? Was it to force the Federals to withdraw troops from the West? Was it some or all of the above?

Admittedly, the truly great commanders in the history of warfare have usually been those who knew when to make exceptions of the rules of war. The Duke of Wellington, by any measure a great captain, was notorious for shaping his offensive strategy from the saddle and for keeping his intentions to himself, even to the extent of providing his lieutenants, including his own brother-in-law, with "Humbug Accounts."[60] Lee, since taking over the command of the Army of Northern Virginia in the spring of 1862, had violated innumerable rules, operating consistently without formal plans. Nevertheless, during the Seven Days, the campaign against Pope, at Fredericksburg, and at Chancellorsville, Lee's objective, if not always clearly stated, had nevertheless been understood: engage, throw back, and if possible destroy the enemy army! Only once, during the Maryland campaign, had Lee undertaken an operation without a clearly defined and broadly understood objective. That campaign ended in near disaster at Sharpsburg. In the summer of 1863, a similar fate awaited the Army of Northern Virginia in Pennsylvania at a small town named Gettysburg.

But why? Two fundamental forces worked against the successful execution of Lee's campaign. First, since Lee's plan, such as it was, existed only in his own mind, it was never properly developed or, to use a modern term, "staffed." Proper planning and staff work identified problems before the beginning of an operation. Those problems could then be anticipated, and in some cases resolved. The failure to staff Lee's plan had dire consequences. Second, Lee relied on a very decentralized approach to command and control. Under normal circumstances, such an approach greatly increased the fighting power of the Army of Northern Virginia, enabling Lee to defeat the much larger Union forces arrayed against him. But Lee's unwillingness to share his concept for the campaign with his principal subordinates undermined the very system that he depended upon to win the victory he sought.

There are two fundamental approaches of command and control available to a commander in his effort to grapple with the problem of uncertainty, often termed in military texts "the fog of war." Those commanders who rely on a centralized approach to command and control issue orders and then closely monitor, or even direct, the actions of their subordinates as they attempt to reach assigned objectives. By centralizing control, a commander achieves greater certainty at the highest level of command—his own—but increases uncertainty at the lower echelons where subordinates, denied initiative, are left periodically without direction. Commanders who employ a more decentralized system identify objectives and then allow subordinates greater leeway in reaching these goals. Decentralized systems accept greater uncertainty at the top, where the commander himself is at times unsure of what is happening, but increase certainty at the lower levels of command where subordinates are able to act decisively on their own initiative. Perhaps the best and most understandable characterization of the decentralized approach was that offered by Vice Admiral Horatio Lord Nelson, who wrote after his great victory at the Nile: "The circumstances of this war so often vary, that an Officer has almost every moment to consider—What would my superiors direct, did they know what is passing under my nose?"[61]

Which system is best? Martin van Creveld, in *Command in War*, his study of command and control, concluded: "If twenty-five centuries of historical experience are any guide, the second way [decentralization] will be superior to the first."[62] Assuming an army has well-motivated and competent officers, a decentralized approach allows those subordinates to take better advantage of situations as they develop on the battlefield. Conversely, for an army led by inexperienced, poorly trained, or incompetent officers, a more centralized system could well be the more effective.

In the eastern theater of operations during the American Civil War, the Union forces arrayed against the Army of Northern Virginia exemplified highly centralized systems of command and control. President Lincoln and General Halleck kept their army commanders in the East on a tight leash, and those generals did the same with their corps commanders. The Duke of Wellington also employed an extremely centralized approach to command during his campaigns in the Iberian Peninsula. He himself acknowledged: "If I detach one of [my lieutenants], he is not satisfied unless I go to him, or send the whole Army; and I am obliged to superintend every operation of the Troops."[63]

By contrast, Robert E. Lee employed an extremely decentralized system of command and control. The relative excellence of his corps, division, and brigade commanders, compared to those of the Federal armies in the eastern theater early in the war, allowed Lee to adopt a far more flexible approach to command and control, one that permitted him to embark on the daring, wide-ranging flanking movements that led to such notable victories as Second Manassas and Chancellorsville. Lee was willing to allow his corps commanders, Longstreet and Jackson, to place themselves in their commander's shoes and to act on their own initiative.

Robert E. Lee was also more comfortable exercising command in a decentralized fashion. Lee disliked having to order subordinates about; he preferred to reason and to suggest, a trait that his biographer Douglas Southall Freeman considered "a positive weakness."[64] With a like-minded subordinate such as Jackson, Lee's approach worked quite well, as it did more generally when the army was on the strategic defensive, whatever the tactical posture of the army. Lee's lieutenants, at the corps, division, and brigade level, understood their mission: hold their ground, repel, and, if possible, destroy the enemy. But for a decentralized system of command and control to function properly on the offensive, even well-motivated and competent subordinates needed to understand the primary goals of a campaign. If, paraphrasing Lord Nelson, Lee's subordinates were to ask themselves, "What would the commanding general direct me to do if he could see what is passing under my nose?" they needed to know the goals of the campaign in order to determine the correct answer to that question. Unfortunately for the Confederacy, during the Maryland and Gettysburg campaigns Lee, intent on keeping the details of his plans secret from the Richmond authorities, was reluctant to share them with his principal subordinate commanders, the one exception being Jackson. During the campaign in Maryland, Lee's unwillingness to confide in his lieutenants had made little difference since the army soon found itself on the defensive along Antietam Creek. But in the Gettysburg campaign, Lee's secretiveness and silence would become a critically important factor affecting the fighting power of the Army of Northern Virginia.[65]

AS THE ARMY SET OUT in early June 1863 on its march toward Gettysburg, the condition and spirit of the troops was extremely high. The degree of straggling was manageable and the number of desertions few. Abram David Pollock, a soldier serving with Brigadier General James L. Kemper's brigade of Virginians, wrote his father: "The contrast between the condition of the army now and last year when we entered Maryland is most encouraging." Pollock and his comrades marched north with "an almost fanatical confidence in their cause & their leader" because, as they said of Lee: "I reckon he knows."[66]

But few, if any, of Lee's subordinates knew their commander's mind. As a result, Lee's corps commanders were unsure what they ought to do at critical points during the campaign. Of Lee's four major commanders—Longstreet, Ewell, Hill, and Stuart—all except Hill committed major errors during the campaign—errors that, in part at least, can be traced to their incomplete understanding of Lee's intentions.

Moreover, after the reorganization of the army in May, several of Lee's principal subordinates lacked the basic competence to act on their own initiative. Ewell and Hill have been the focus of historical criticism, and a consensus exists that they were both men who ought never to have commanded anything larger than a division. Lee's unwillingness to share his plans with them exacerbated their shortcomings.

Even Lee's competent lieutenants found themselves facing difficult choices with a less than complete understanding of their commander's intentions. Perhaps the best example involved Jeb Stuart's decision to conduct his infamous ride around the Army of the Potomac during the Gettysburg campaign.

By the summer of 1863, Stuart, a thirty-year-old graduate of West Point (class of 1854), was the epitome of the dashing Rebel cavalryman. The hard-driving and hard-fighting Stuart was well loved by his troopers and his scouting and screening services were much appreciated by his commander and fellow Virginian—Robert E. Lee. Stuart's most noteworthy feat had been his famous "ride" around McClellan's army during the Peninsula campaign of 1862.

Unfortunately for Stuart, his attempt to repeat his success the following year gained him infamy rather than fame. Lee linked Stuart's failure to provide accurate and timely intelligence concerning the movements of the Federals to the inability of the commander of the Army of Northern Virginia to avoid battle at Gettysburg.[67] As Harry Heth, commander of a division in A. P. Hill's Third Corps later wrote, in the days before the battle Lee often expressed his concerns about Stuart's absence, because "the eyes and ears of his army were absent."[68] Lee himself noted in his July 31 report that "the absence of cavalry rendered it impossible to obtain accurate information."[69] And in January 1864 Lee wrote that it had been "expected that as soon as the Federal Army should cross the Potomac, General Stuart would give notice of its movements."[70] Colonel Long recalled in his memoir that on the eve of Gettysburg, Lee lamented the fact that "he had been kept in the dark ever since crossing the Potomac, and intimated that Stuart's disappearance had materially hampered the movements and disorganized the plans of the campaign."[71] In a postwar conversation with William Allan, Lee was also critical of Stuart. Lee, Allan noted, "did not know the Federal army was at Gettysburg, *could not believe it,* as Stuart had been specially ordered to cover his (Lee's) movement & keep him informed of the position of the enemy, & he (Stuart) had sent no word. . . . Stuart's failure to carry out his instructions *forced the battle of Gettysburg.*"[72] In Lee's exposition of the Gettysburg campaign, Stuart's failures played a role akin to that of the Lost Dispatch in the Maryland campaign—the misfortune that led to an unfortunate and unsuccessful battle.

Not surprisingly, many historians have accepted Lee's view on the matter and have criticized Stuart. Douglas Southall Freeman attributed Stuart's decision less to good, or even questionable sense, than to a desire to recoup the personal and popular prestige lost when the Federal cavalry surprised the Confederate horsemen on June 9, 1863, at Brandy Station.[73]

Whatever Stuart's personal motivations, Lee must bear the primary responsibility for whatever missteps ensued. To be sure, it was Stuart who first proposed the plan.[74] But Lee, despite his concerns, refused to issue a direct order and chose to permit his vainglorious subordinate to act upon his own initiative. Nor did Lee provide Stuart with a clearly defined framework within which a decision could be made. Lee wrote Stuart on June 23:

> If General Hooker's army remains inactive, you can leave two brigades to watch him, and withdraw with the three others [and ride around the army], but should he not appear to be moving northward, I think you had better withdraw this side of the mountain to-morrow night, cross at Shepherdstown next day, and move over to Fredericktown.
>
> You will, however, be able to judge whether you can pass around their army without hindrance, doing them all the damage you can, and cross the river east of the mountains. In either case, after crossing the river, you must move on and feel for the right of Ewell's troops, collecting information, provisions, &c.[75]

What, exactly, did Lee mean? If Hooker was not moving northward, could he not then be considered "inactive"?[76] And what was Stuart's primary responsibility: doing the Federals "damage," collecting provisions, or taking a position on the right flank of Ewell's corps, which had already been operating north of the Potomac without a proper cavalry screen for eight days?

In a post-campaign report on the operations of the cavalry that was more detailed and longer than Lee's for the entire army, Stuart remained unrepentant, even to the point of contradicting a statement made by his commander in his own July 31 report. From Stuart's account it appears that he assumed that the campaign was intended primarily to forage and to harass, not to seek battle. He also made a point that has been overlooked by most historians. He wrote: " . . . the route I took was quite as direct and more expeditious than the alternate one proposed."[77]

On June 23, as Stuart reviewed his options, the major problem he confronted was one of traffic management. Lee's cavalry had three distinct roles to fulfill during the campaign. During the initial phase it had to screen the army's movements across Virginia and down the Shenandoah Valley. In the second, trans-Potomac phase, the cavalry had not only to screen and scout, but also to forage widely in search for supplies. Stuart's problem was that the execution of his mission in the first phase of the campaign left him at the rear of the army, whereas during the second phase he was expected to suddenly take up a position in the van. How, exactly, was Stuart to accomplish this? He had two options: to ride, with three brigades of horsemen, either around the Army of the Potomac or through much of the Army of Northern Virginia. Lee preferred the former option, and suggested that Stuart cross the Potomac at Shepherdstown on June 25. But, as one of Stuart's staff officers wrote, "All the roads leading northward through the valley were densely filled with the trains of artillery, and quartermaster, commissary and ordnance wagons, to say nothing of the infantry columns."[78] Had Stuart chosen to follow Lee's suggestion, he would have found the valley roads leading to the fords near Shepherdstown filled with the soldiers, guns, and wagons of Hill's Third Corps, which crossed there on June 24 and 25. To the west, Longstreet's First Corps was crossing at Williamsport on the twenty-fifth and twenty-sixth. If Stuart had been able to cross at Shepherdstown on the twenty-sixth, and had he followed Lee's directions and continued on toward Frederick in an effort to "feel" for Ewell's right flank, the Rebel cavalry would have encountered the Federal troops who arrived there on the twenty-seventh. Despite Lee's assertions, it was impossible for Stuart, positioned as he was, to have discovered the initial Federal crossing of the Potomac on June 25, although Lee might have learned of the Federal advance into Maryland perhaps a half day earlier than he actually did.

Given the limited number of crossing points along the Potomac, and the handful of roads leading north, had Lee's plan of campaign been properly developed and staffed, Stuart's dilemma would—or at least should—have been foreseen. Lee should have planned to have one of Stuart's five cavalry brigades accompany Ewell into Maryland when he crossed the Potomac on June 15.[79]

Instead, infantry led Lee's advance north, just as the infantry had led the advance into Maryland in September 1862, while Stuart's cavalry formed the army's rear guard. And once again an unexpected Federal advance upset Lee's plans. While Lee, as he claimed in his reports, was without accurate intelligence concerning the movements of the Army of the Potomac during the days before the battle of Gettysburg, his allegation that the condition was the result of Stuart's absence is a distortion of the historical record. From the beginning of the campaign, Lee had been groping about, uncertain of the positions and movements of the Federal army.

The problem was that the Union cavalry was operating far more efficiently than it had in the past. At Brandy Station, Stuart had been taken aback by the tenacity of the Union attacks. "The Federal cavalry," Freeman wrote, "never had battled so hard and never had stood up so stubbornly."[80] While Stuart had successfully screened the movements of the Army of Northern Virginia, the Federal cavalry had been just as successful in its attempts to shield the movements of the Army of the Potomac. In a June 19 letter to Ewell, written well before Stuart embarked on his ride, Lee admitted that he had no idea of where Hooker was moving.[81] On June 22, Lee asked Stuart: "Do you know where [Hooker] is and what he is doing? I fear he will steal a march on us, and get across the Potomac before we are aware."[82]

The Federals did, in fact, "steal a march." They started across the Potomac near Leesburg late on June 25. The Army of the Potomac was across the river and generally moving west with its van in Frederick by the twenty-seventh. The march north toward Pennsylvania did not begin until the twenty-ninth.[83]

On the night of June 28, reports reached Lee at his head-quarters in Chambersburg, Pennsylvania, that the Federals, now commanded by Major General George Gordon Meade, were across the river and in Frederick, about thirty-five miles to the southeast, moving westward as if to threaten Lee's communications with the valley and Virginia. Lee, like Wellington before the battle of Waterloo, had been "hum bugged." The Confederate general had failed to keep Napoleon's eighth maxim in mind:

> A general-in-chief should ask himself frequently in the day, What should I do if the enemy's army appeared now in my front, or on my right, or on my left? If he [has] any difficulty in answering these questions, he is ill posted and should seek to remedy it.[84]

Lee had, once again, underestimated an opponent. Hooker had reacted more quickly than Lee had hoped, or expected, just as McClellan had the previous summer. Lee had entered Maryland in 1862 planning a campaign about the countryside for three to four weeks before being challenged. Thirteen days after his first troops crossed the Potomac he was fighting for survival at Sharpsburg. Nine months later Lee marched north again, expecting to operate in Pennsylvania throughout the summer before returning to Virginia in the fall. Sixteen days after Ewell's

van crossed the river, the Army of Northern Virginia found itself engaged in an epic battle at Gettysburg. The fault was not
Jeb Stuart's.

STUART WAS NOT the only senior commander of the Army of
Northern Virginia whose decisions caused Lee concern in late
June 1863. Ewell faltered before Winchester; while Longstreet,
who had supported Seddon's calls for part, or all, of the First
Corps to be sent west, did not share Lee's vision of the forth-
coming campaign.

The forty-six-year old Richard Stoddert Ewell, grandson of
the first secretary of the navy, was another Virginian and West
Point graduate (class of 1840). Ewell had served on the frontier
and in the Mexican War, and after joining the Confederacy became one of the most dependable division commanders in the
Army of Northern Virginia, serving with distinction under Jackson in the Shenandoah Valley, during the Seven Days, and the
campaign against Pope. But as "Old Bald Head," as Ewell was
known to some of his soldiers, led a counterattack during the
battle of Groveton on August 28, 1862, he was felled by a ball
that shattered his right knee. The surgeons had to amputate the
leg above the knee, and he spent the next nine months recovering from his wound.

Ewell returned to duty in late May as a lieutenant general,
commander of Jackson's Second Corps, but a changed man,
both physically and emotionally. He had written Jubal Early in
March, expressing his hope that the war would end in the
spring before he completed his recovery: "I don't want to see
the carnage and shocking sights of another field of battle,
though I prefer being in the field to anywhere else as long as
the war is going on."[85] Even in May, the physical effects of his
wound were still with him. Because the stump caused him pain,
Ewell was often forced to remove his wooden leg and instead
to go about on crutches or in a coach. One soldier who saw Old
Bald Head on his return to the army noted that he was "look-

ing quite badly."[86] Ewell had also gained a wife and found religion during his convalescence. As a result, the new Ewell had lost some of his former irascibility and his propensity to swear, but many of his friends were also convinced that he was "not the same soldier he had been when a whole man and a single one."[87]

John Brown Gordon, who served under Ewell in a variety of capacities, considered him "the most unique personality I have ever known."[88] Ewell's "written orders were full, accurate, and lucid; but his verbal orders or directions, especially when under intense excitement, no man could comprehend. At times his eyes would flash with a peculiar brilliancy, and his brain far outran his tongue."[89]

Lee had doubts about Ewell's suitability for corps command. The army commander had known Ewell before the war and believed him to be subject to "quick alterations from elation to despondency" and "want of decision."[90] In fact, at First Manassas, Ewell had refused to launch an attack on the Federals without direct orders, despite the fact that even he believed that the moment for an assault was at hand.[91] Ewell had nevertheless performed well under Jackson, although always under his direct command or in response to clearly written orders. Ewell had never yet operated under Lee's direction and rather different style of command. Lee, fearing that Ewell might regress to "the old habit . . . talked earnestly with him when he assumed command."[92]

As fortune had it, Ewell bore the difficult responsibility of leading the advance into Pennsylvania. After the battle of Chancellorsville, the Second Corps lay on the left wing of the army; Hill's Third Corps was on the right. The divisions of Longstreet, Lee's most experienced corps commander, were still moving toward Culpeper when the army began its march in early June.

Initially, Ewell's management of his corps in the movements westward across Virginia and then down the valley was exemplary. Stonewall Jackson himself could not have performed better. Freeman, in *Lee's Lieutenants,* entitled the chapter on Ewell's march "As If a Second Jackson Had Come."[93] Nevertheless, Lee caught a glimpse of the "old habit." He told William Allan in 1868 that

> after he had sent Ewell ahead, and given him full instructions, and told him that he had sent him ahead confiding in his judgment, and that he must be guided by his own judgment in any unforeseen emergency, that at Winchester Ewell, after sending him very encouraging messages about entrapping Milroy, and detailing Rode's & Early's movements, suddenly sent a dispatch stating that upon closer inspection he found the works too strong to be attacked, and asking his (Lee's) instructions![94]

If Lee entered Pennsylvania with doubts about Ewell's suitability to direct the operations of a corps, the commander of the Army of Northern Virginia also had concerns about the state of mind of Lieutenant General James Longstreet. His conduct during the subsequent battle would become one of the most divisive topics among Confederate memoirists, and ultimately among historians.[95]

After the war, Longstreet portrayed himself as a man who had not shared, but feared the consequences of, Lee's views on Confederate grand strategy, strategy in the eastern theater, operations, and tactics. In the spring of 1863 Longstreet did, in fact, oppose Lee's plan for a Northern invasion and support proposals, such as those put forth by Secretary of War Seddon, calling for a detachment of troops—usually Longstreet's—from Lee's army for service in the West. Lee, of course, forcefully opposed these calls on his command, and no doubt resented Longstreet's behavior.[96] Nevertheless, as Jeffry D. Wert demonstrated in his critical biography of Longstreet, what the lieutenant general did not mention in his postwar writings was that he had become a decided convert to the idea of an invasion of Pennsylvania after meeting with his commander.[97] Like Davis and Seddon, Longstreet succumbed that spring to the charms and arguments of Robert E. Lee.

Nevertheless, while Lee convinced Longstreet of the efficacy of a strategic offensive, the two generals did not agree on the role of battle, nor on the character of an engagement should one be fought during the course of the campaign. Longstreet's postwar claim that he had wrung a promise from Lee not to adopt a tactically offensive posture—that is, not to attack a Federal army in the field, but to maneuver the army offensively into a position that would force a Federal assault—was much overblown. In 1868, Lee termed Longstreet's claim "absurd."[98] Still, the two men were not of one mind with regard to battle.

As a result, while the commander of the First Corps was now Lee's senior and most experienced lieutenant, there never developed between Longstreet and Lee a personal rapport comparable to that which had existed between Jackson and Lee. That is not to say that Lee did not come to rely more heavily on Longstreet than he did his other corps commanders and often take him into his confidence. But, as the course of the campaign would demonstrate, Longstreet did not know Lee's mind as had Jackson.

As the Army of Northern Virginia marched toward the Potomac, Longstreet soon revealed his ignorance of Lee's plans and intentions. While Ewell's Second Corps drove down the valley and across the Potomac, Longstreet's First Corps was supposed to operate east of the Blue Ridge Mountains, along with Jeb Stuart, both to screen the movements of the army and to pose a threat to Washington that, Lee hoped, would hold Hooker south of the river as long as possible.[99] In several dispatches, Lee directed the movements of the First Corps along the eastern slope of the mountains. Nevertheless, Longstreet, on his own initiative, marched his men into the valley. As he wrote in his report of the campaign:

> I received a dispatch from general headquarters, directing that I should hold myself in readiness to move in the direction of the Potomac, with a view to crossing, &c. As I was ready, and had been expecting an order to execute such purpose, I supposed the intimation meant other preparation, and, knowing

of nothing else that I could do to render my preparations complete, I supposed that it was desirable that I should cross the Shenandoah. I therefore passed the river, occupied the banks at the ferries opposite the Gaps, and a road at an intermediate ford, which was practicable for cavalry and infantry.[100]

This was not what Lee had in mind, and when the commanding general learned of Longstreet's movements he wrote:

If a part of our force could have operated east of the mountains, it would have served more to confuse [Hooker], but as you have turned off to the Valley, and I understand all the trains have taken that route, I hope it is for the best. At any rate, it is too late to change from any information I have. You had better, therefore, push on, relieve Ewell's division as soon as you can, and let him advance into Maryland, at least as far as Hagerstown.[101]

Did Longstreet's misstep allow Hooker to cross the Potomac earlier than he would otherwise have? Probably not, although no one can say for certain. But the often overlooked incident demonstrates quite clearly that even Longstreet, Lee's most trusted commander, did not know—or at least did not fully understand—what Robert E. Lee was doing. And if James Longstreet did not know, who, if anyone, did?

LIEUTENANT GENERAL A. P. HILL was the only one of Lee's four principal lieutenants whose conduct during the initial phase of the operation offered no reason for censure. An outnumbered Third Corps held the Federals at bay at Fredericksburg while Lee sidestepped the rest of the army westward. When the proper time arrived, Hill hustled his own men through Culpeper and into the valley. Powell Hill seemed to be as comfortable in command of a corps as he had been in his direction of the famed Light Division.

But Hill's moment was soon to arrive. On June 28, when Lee learned that the Federals were at Frederick, he ordered a reconcentration of the army that brought elements of the Second and Third Corps toward the small Pennsylvania town of Gettysburg. Ewell's men were coming down from the north, while Hill's were marching east, through Cashtown.

Major General Harry Heth's division was in the van of Hill's corps, scouting—or more accurately, groping—ahead in the absence of Stuart's cavalry. On June 30, Heth sent Brigadier General James J. Pettigrew's brigade into Gettysburg in search of supplies, particularly shoes. Pettigrew's North Carolinians found no footwear, but discovered the presence of some Union cavalry and promptly withdrew.

Pettigrew was reporting his encounter when Powell Hill arrived at Heth's headquarters. Hill, basing his opinions on earlier discussions with Lee, believed that the Federals were moving west, and not north. The Federal horsemen in Gettysburg, he reasoned, were nothing more than a scouting party. That being the case, Heth wished to march back to the town, this time with his whole division. Hill agreed.[102] Only Pettigrew disagreed, and later protested, but Hill refused to change his order, for he doubted that any sizable force of Yankees were present. But, Pettigrew wondered, what if there was a strong force of Federals in Gettysburg? Hill told his brigadier: "I hope that it is, for this is the place I want it to be."[103]

The next morning, July 1, found Hill quite ill with much of the fire of the previous day extinguished by fever and discomfort. As Heth moved his division down the road toward Gettysburg, he received a last-minute cautionary order from his sick commander: "Do not bring on an engagement."[104] But it was too late. Heth's leading brigades stumbled into a virtual ambush, were mauled by two brigades of Union cavalry, and then all but destroyed by the counterattack of two divisions of the Army of the Potomac's First Corps. Heth brought up the rest of his division in support and, not wishing to bring on a general engagement, waited for further direction from Hill.

Hill, somewhat invigorated by the sound of battle, was once more the aggressive commander of the Light Division. With

Major General William Dorsey Pender's division up in support of Heth, Hill was prepared to renew the assault. He instructed Heth and Pender to prepare their men for an advance. But then Lee arrived. He listened as Heth and Hill explained the situation, and then decided against an immediate assault. If the infantry of the Federal First Corps was up, the rest of the Army of the Potomac had to be close at hand. But where? And in what strength? And where was Ewell? Or Stuart? Lee announced that he did not wish to bring on a general engagement until more of his own army reached the field.

About 2:30 P.M. Heth heard the staccato crackle of musketry from the northeast. Major General Robert Rodes's division of Ewell's corps had reached the field and crashed into the right flank of the Union line north of Gettysburg. Heth rushed to Lee and asked for permission to advance, but the army commander refused. "I do not wish to bring on a general engagement to-day," he advised Heth. "Longstreet is not up."[105] But when Heth returned to the line, he could see the Federals shifting forces from his idle front to the north of the town to oppose Rodes, now joined by Early's division. Heth rode off to find Lee and again explained the situation. "Wait awhile," Lee advised, "and I will send you word when to go in."[106] Lee's hand had been forced. He directed Hill to send Heth and Pender forward to support Ewell. The battle of Gettysburg, whether Lee wanted one or not, had become general.

Despite Heth's bungled advance in the morning, and comparable errors committed by Rodes north of the town, the Confederates achieved a notable battlefield success on the afternoon of July 1, driving the Federals back from their positions north and west of Gettysburg. Considering the fact that both Hill and Ewell were making their debuts as corps commanders, they performed competently, if not expertly. Hill's orders may have confused Heth to a degree, but it seems unfair to blame the commander of the Third Corps for forcing Lee into a battle he did not wish to fight. In fact, one could more easily criticize Lee for hesitating to send Heth and Pender forward when Rodes first began his assault.

But if the sins of commission, or omission, committed during the morning and early afternoon of July 1 by senior Confederate commanders were understandable and excusable, not so those of the late afternoon. As Rodes's and Early's brigades drove the retreating Federals south through Gettysburg, they were poised to continue their advance and to seize the high ground that lay before them—East Cemetery and Culp's Hills. But Ewell held up the advance. Dumbfounded, Gordon—commanding a brigade in Early's division—rode to see Ewell and pressed him for permission to attack. Ewell refused. Just then Major Henry Kyd Douglas, the assistant adjutant general (effectively chief of staff) of Ewell's third and still uncommitted division, that of Major General Edward Johnson, rode up and announced that Johnson would soon be up and would be prepared to go into action immediately. Gordon asked for permission to attack when Johnson came up, but again Ewell refused. "General Lee told me to come to Gettysburg and gave me orders to go no further," Ewell replied. "I do not feel like advancing and making an attack without orders from him, and he is back at Cashtown."[107] Johnson's men would come into line, but would not advance without orders. At this, Major A. S. "Sandy" Pendleton, Ewell's own chief of staff, was said to have muttered: "Oh, for the presence and inspiration of Old Jack for just one hour!"[108] Douglas himself later wrote that "it took the battle of Gettysburg to convince General Lee that General Jackson was really dead."[109]

As the daylight waned, the pressure on Ewell continued to mount. Major General Isaac R. Trimble, the commander of the Valley District who was serving as a supernumerary with the army, rode up and asked why Ewell's men were not pressing the Federals and exploiting the victory. Ewell explained that Lee did not wish to bring on a general engagement, and that Second Corps would go no further without orders. Trimble rode off, but returned again. The Federals were strengthening the hills, he warned, and the opportunity to seize them was slipping away. And with regard to a general engagement, what, Trimble wondered, had just been fought if not a general engagement? But Ewell would not relent.

Next it was Jubal Early's turn, and at last Ewell, visibly agitated, began to weaken. Ewell agreed to attack, but only if he could secure an order from Lee and if Powell Hill would launch a simultaneous assault from the west.[110]

Just then Major Taylor arrived from the army staff with a message from Lee, who was himself on the way. The actual order did not survive the battle, so the details of what it contained are the subject of some degree of dispute. Ewell wrote in his report of the battle:

> The enemy had fallen back to a commanding position known as Cemetery Hill, south of Gettysburg, and quickly showed a formidable front there. On entering the town, I received a message from the commanding general to attack this hill, if I could do so to advantage. I could not bring artillery to bear on it, and all the troops with me were jaded by twelve hours marching and fighting, and I was notified that General Johnson's division (the only one of my corps that had not been engaged) was close to the town.
>
> Cemetery Hill was not assailable from the town, and I determined, with Johnson's division, to take possession of a wooded hill to my left, on a line with and commanding Cemetery Hill. Before Johnson got up, the enemy was reported moving to outflank our extreme left, and I could see what seemed to be his skirmishers in that direction.[111]

Lee wrote of the same order:

> General Ewell was, therefore, instructed to carry the hill occupied by the enemy, if he found it practicable, but to avoid a general engagement until the arrival of the other divisions of the army, which were ordered to hasten forward. He decided to await Johnson's division, which had marched from

Carlisle by the road west of the mountains to guard the trains of his corps, and consequently did not reach Gettysburg until a late hour.[112]

Ewell, besieged by his subordinates and staff, now mulled over his situation. Lee's order was hardly succinct. What was more important: taking the hill or avoiding a general engagement? As Ewell considered his options, another messenger arrived from Lee: Hill's corps would not assist the effort. Ewell decided to reconnoiter the Federal positions, to wait for Johnson to come up, and for Lee to arrive. But by then it was too late.

Historians have been rightly critical of Ewell's inaction on the late afternoon of July 1. There can be no doubt that he ought to have directed Early and Rodes to continue their drive south of the town and to seize the two hills. What impact such an action, assuming it was successful, would have had on the course of the battle can never be known.

What is also clear is that Lee's command methods all but ensured failure on the afternoon of the first day at Gettysburg. The decentralized approach to command and control that served Lee so well on other occasions failed him on July 1 because the two elements necessary to make the system work—competent subordinates, and clearly defined and enunciated plans and objectives—were lacking. Ewell, as Lee had feared and should have known after Winchester, was no Stonewall Jackson. Despite the fact that Lee had ordered the army to concentrate around Gettysburg, Ewell was clearly confused about whether or not Lee wished to actually fight a battle there. What Lee needed to do late in the afternoon of July 1 was to take command of his own army. Lee was a West Pointer, a trained engineering officer. He could see the high ground south of the town and appreciate its importance. All he needed to do was to direct—to order—both Ewell and Hill to advance. Instead, Lee asked Hill if he could attack; Hill, tired and sick, declined.[113] Lee's orders to Ewell, as they are reflected in the commanding general's report, were cautionary in the extreme and hardly direct.

Why did Lee fail to issue the necessary orders? The reasons are two: first, to issue such direct orders would, of course, have been out of character; and second, on the afternoon of July 1, Lee himself did not know whether or not he wished to bring on a general engagement. Not until the evening did he finally decide to continue the battle. As he reasoned in his preliminary report:

> It had not been intended to fight a general battle at such a distance from our base, unless attacked by the enemy, but, finding ourselves unexpectedly confronted by the Federal Army, it became a matter of difficulty to withdraw through the mountains with our large trains. At the same time, the country was unfavorable for collecting supplies while in the presence of the enemy's main body, as he was enabled to restrain our foraging parties by occupying the passes of the mountains with regular and local troops. A battle thus became, in a measure, unavoidable. Encouraged by the successful issue of the engagement of the first day, and in view of the valuable results that would ensue from the defeat of the army of General Meade, it was thought advisable to renew the attack.[114]

Lee, in his late afternoon effort to pass the responsibility for continuing the battle to Ewell and Hill, was avoiding his own accountability as commander.

LEE, HAVING FINALLY DECIDED to fight his "general engagement," needed, as soon as possible—preferably before dawn—to formulate a plan of action for the coming day. This he failed to do, in part because of his uncertainty about the enemy's positions, but also because of a lack of cooperation on the part of his corps commanders. Ewell and his division commanders were reluctant to yield the ground they had won and to move during the night from their lines east of Gettysburg to new positions south and west of the town on Hill's immediate left.[115] Lee's unwillingness to order Ewell to move ensured that it would be extremely difficult for the commanding general to coordinate the movements of Ewell, on the far left, and Long-street, who was coming up on the far right. Nor was Longstreet particularly cooperative. Lee wanted the First Corps to attack on the right, but Longstreet, who believed that it was a mistake to assume the tactical offensive, objected. He proposed instead that the entire army maneuver around the Federal left flank.[116] Lee insisted; meanwhile, more time slipped away, and with it went the opportunity for the generals to rest before the coming action. Lee rode off, leaving Longstreet angered and disap-pointed.[117]

It was midmorning before Lee had finalized his plan. Long-street would launch the main attack with two divisions—those of Major Generals Lafayette McLaws and John Bell Hood—against the Federal left and roll up Meade's flank. Ewell would launch his attack in support and, if practicable, seize the hills before him. Lee set no deadlines; both attacks would com-mence when the respective commanders believed the troops were ready.

Unfortunately, Ewell grew tired of waiting for Longstreet. He attacked on his own and, worse yet, proved himself inca-pable of coordinating the actions of his three divisions. Each struck the Federals in turn, and to little effect. Lee later told William Allan that Ewell could not "act with decision" and that as a result, Rodes, Early, and Johnson "attacked and were hurt in detail."[118]

Nevertheless, Lee had not expected much from Ewell's at-tack; the main assault was to come on the Confederate right flank. But as the hours passed, and Longstreet's attack failed to materialize, Lee became increasingly agitated. In his reports on the battle, he made no mention of any delay on Longstreet's part, but memoirists, especially those who served on Lee's staff, accused the First Corps commander of an unnecessary delay that may have cost the Confederacy the battle—and to some minds, the war.[119] Longstreet, in his own memoirs, claimed that he moved as promptly as possible and blamed the delay on Lee's failure to issue his orders more promptly.[120] But G. Moxley

Sorrel, the First Corps chief of staff, accused Longstreet of "apathy" in his preparation for the attack, rooted in his dislike for Lee's plan.[121] Jeffry D. Wert, whose biography of Longstreet provides an excellent reconstruction of the timeline of Lee's decisions, concluded that Longstreet "deserves censure for the performance on the morning of July 2. He allowed his disagreement with Lee's decision to affect his conduct."[122]

But while Ewell's incompetence and Longstreet's recalcitrance were important factors, Lee's unwillingness to issue direct orders or to take charge of the battle lay at the root of the problem. He left the timing of the First Corps attack up to Longstreet, who saw fit to delay until 4:00 P.M. By then more Federal troops were in position, and there were too few hours remaining in the day to exploit fully a marked success, had one been gained. As on the first day of the battle, Lee's style of command and lack of direction ensured that his subordinates failed to make the most of the opportunities that lay before the Army of Northern Virginia.

It was not until the third day of the battle that Lee actually took charge, although by then the prospects of victory were few. The entire Federal army was now in position, dug in along a series of ridges and hills. Given the situation, the most sensible courses of action for Lee would have been to withdraw or to go over to the defensive and hope that the enemy would attack, a tactically sensible but logistically difficult option. Lee, of course, chose a third option: to assault the center of the Federal line— the infamous "Pickett's Charge."

No one can ever say with certainty why Lee ordered what, in retrospect, appears to have been a senseless, even suicidal assault. But consider Lee's determination to attack as but the last of a series of decisions stretching back to early April 1863. Recall the promises that Lee had made to Davis, Seddon, and the cabinet about the supposed benefits of a Northern invasion. Do not overlook the incredible burdens that Lee had placed on his own shoulders and those of his men—not just to perform well, not simply to harass the Yankees, not solely to save Richmond for another campaigning season, but also to redress the imbalance of forces in the western theater, and, perhaps, even to win the war. How could Lee, his army as yet undefeated, possibly recross the Potomac River and return to Virginia empty-handed without having struck one final blow? Just as a worried Lee had felt compelled to cross the river a week earlier, he now felt compelled to stake all on a forlorn hope. When Pickett's Charge failed, Lee knew that he had lost more than a few thousand men, more than a battle, even more than his own campaign. As the survivors, battered and beaten, made their way back toward their lines, Lee spoke the truth when he lamented: "It is all my fault."

IN FACT, LEE'S INVASION PLAN had failed well before Pickett's Charge. At Gettysburg, Lee was attempting to salvage on the battlefield a campaign that, much akin to the Maryland campaign of 1862, had not proceeded as expected. As Major Taylor of Lee's staff admitted to his brother, "[H]ad we been eminently successful at Gettysburg, in all probability we would have been obliged to make the same movements we have."[123] Fortunately for Lee, once again the failure of a Federal commander—this time Meade—to pursue aggressively allowed the Army of Northern Virginia to avoid destruction. Nonetheless, the cost had been high. Federal casualties totaled 23,001; those of the Confederates, 20,448.[124]

The question that now remained to be answered was: what lessons would Lee draw from his second failed strategic offensive? Just as he had paid little heed to many of the lessons that he might have drawn from the Maryland campaign, he now chose to ignore those of the Gettysburg campaign. He downplayed, to an incredible degree, the significance of his failures, and not just in the official reports already cited. In a July 12 letter to his wife, Lee displayed his well developed talent for understatement, writing: "You will have learned before this reaches you that our success at Gettysburg was not as great as reported. In fact, we failed to drive the enemy from his position & that our army withdrew to the Potomac."[125] Three days later, with the army back across the Potomac a month to the day after Rodes first crossed the river, Lee wrote again, admitting that his return to Virginia had come "sooner than I had originally contemplated, but having accomplished what I purposed on leaving the Rappahannock, viz., relieving the Valley of the presence of the enemy & drawing his army north of the Potomac, I determined to recross the latter river."[126] The campaign was at an end, but not Lee's desire to resume the offensive.

3

The Bristoe Station Campaign

"The Saddest Chapter in the History of this Army"

LEE'S ARMY RETREATED FROM GETTYSBURG in fairly good form, but in bad spirits. Thousands of comrades lay dead on the fields surrounding the Pennsylvania town.[1] Few senior Confederate officers emerged from the battle with enhanced reputations. In Richmond, press and politicians wondered, Who was responsible for the myriad errors that led to such a disastrous defeat?[2] How had the dynamic mood of the spring—the spirit of Chancellorsville—been so quickly dissipated? As commander of the army, Lee bore the responsibility and shouldered the guilt himself. He rode toward Virginia planning to resign once the army safely returned to Southern soil.

By August 4, the Army of Northern Virginia was across the Rapidan River. Despite the disappointing events of the summer, morale slowly began to improve.[3] Commanders worked diligently to check desertions while officials in the rear sought to bring the army up to strength.[4] But replacements were few, reinforcements fewer, desertions continued to be a problem, supplies were not reaching the front, thousands of men were unarmed, and the army's horses had no fodder.[5] The Army of

Northern Virginia remained weak and poorly equipped.[6] On August 8, Lee tendered his resignation to President Jefferson Davis.[7]

Lee's offer did not come at a particularly opportune time for Davis. July 1863 had been the worst month of the war for the Confederacy. War Department clerk Jones noted that Davis's health was poor, and Secretary of War Seddon, "who usually wears a sallow and cadaverous look, which, coupled with his emaciation makes him resemble an exhumed corpse after a month's internment, looks today like a galvanized corpse which had been buried for two months."[8] As bleak as Confederate prospects looked in northern Virginia, the situation elsewhere was worse. Despite Lee's promises, his invasion of the North had failed to force the Federals to draw off troops from the other theaters for service in Pennsylvania and Maryland. As a result, the South reeled under heavy blows both east and west. Union forces threatened to drive inland from their enclaves along the coasts of North and South Carolina. The Federals controlled the entire length of the Mississippi and were driving eastward through Tennessee. Since Davis had few men capable of army command waiting in the wings, Lee, whatever his faults, was far more competent than the other senior Confederate commanders. As the president wrote on August 11: "But suppose my dear friend, that I were to admit, with all their implications, the points which you present [Lee's lamentations about his increasingly poor health and shortcomings as a general], where am I to find that new commander who is to possess the greater ability which you believe to be required?"[9]

Davis's most pressing concern was to find a way to reverse the current course of military events. The continued Union offensive in the West threatened the heart of the Confederacy. There was a growing consensus among senior Southern leaders, both civilian and military, that their armies could not remain passively on the defensive. Confederate forces had to deliver a counterstroke, somewhere, to arrest the Federal advance.

Since the most immediate and severe threat lay in the West, where Union troops, victorious at Vicksburg, continued to advance, the logical response was to mount an offensive in Tennessee to throw back, or at least to check, Federal progress. But General Braxton Bragg's Army of Tennessee was too weak to do the job itself and would have to be reinforced. Once again, Seddon began to view Lee's Army of Northern Virginia as the most likely source for such detachments.

The idea of sending several of Lee's divisions west was a topic of conversation not only in Richmond, but also in Lee's headquarters. In mid August Longstreet, commander of Lee's own First Corps, wrote Secretary of War Seddon once again proposing the use of the South's "interior lines" to transfer troops from Lee's army westward to strike Major General William S. Rosecrans's Army of the Cumberland before it delivered "the finishing stroke of the war."[10]

In late August, President Davis once again called Lee, his hand weakened by his failure at Gettysburg, to Richmond for consultations.[11] He knew that there was growing sentiment to transfer units from the East to the West. Why not use the South's central position—interior lines—to shift troops between theaters? Why not do on the grand strategic level what Confederate commanders, among them Lee himself, had done in the East—moving troops between the coastal region and the Shenandoah Valley?[12] But the general, who had already discussed the troop transfer scheme with Longstreet, was no more eager to detach units from his army than he had been in April or May. Lee remained adamant. As the authors of *Why the South Lost the Civil War* noted, Davis "had run into an example of what [Carl von] Clausewitz called a commander's feeling of 'proprietary right' over all of his troops and the usual objection 'to any part being withdrawn for however short a time.'"[13] Despite the deteriorating situation in the West, Lee opposed detaching units from his army and believed that the best way to relieve the pressure on Bragg was for the Army of Northern Virginia to resume the offensive. Less than two months after the disastrous defeat at Gettysburg, Lee wanted to attack.[14]

Once again, Lee's powers of persuasion carried the day, despite the fact that his April assurances about an invasion being the best way to save Vicksburg had proven unfounded.[15] In Richmond on August 30, War Department clerk Jones wrote in his diary: "Gen. Lee has returned to the Army of Northern Virginia—and we shall probably soon hear of interesting operations in the field."[16] On August 31, Lee sent a confidential letter to Longstreet, who commanded the army in Lee's absence, to "use every exertion to prepare the army for offensive operations."[17]

Longstreet doubted the wisdom of such a move, writing Lee that "I do not know that we can reasonably hope to accomplish much here by offensive operations, unless you are strong enough to cross the Potomac. If we advance to meet the enemy on this side, he will, in all probability, go into one of his many fortified positions; these we cannot afford to attack."[18] Longstreet then restated his earlier suggestion of a shift of operations to Tennessee.

While most of the Army of Northern Virginia's rank and file, especially the Virginians and North Carolinians, had little desire to go west, they had even less interest in another invasion of the North. Captain Thomas Jackson Strayhorn of the Twenty-seventh North Carolina Infantry Regiment wrote: "I think the Battle of Sharpsburg ought to have taught us a lesson. We have no business invading the enemy's country. We can effect but little and we endanger ourselves by it."[19] Another North Carolina soldier noted after Gettysburg: "I never want to go to Maryland nor Penn any more but I am fearful we are going right back."[20]

But unbeknownst to Longstreet, to clerk Jones, or to the soldiers of the Army of Northern Virginia, developments in the West were forcing Davis to reconsider his initial decision to allow Lee to attack Meade. On September 2, Federal troops captured Knoxville, and the fall of Chattanooga appeared imminent. Davis had to recast his plans. There was nothing Lee could do in Virginia that could possibly check Rosecrans before the city fell. On September 3, before the commander of the Army of Northern Virginia left the capital, an exhausted Davis met again with Lee. The two men rode together through the streets of the Confederate capital, to few cheers.[21] Davis directed his reluctant subordinate to begin the transfer of troops to reinforce Bragg's Army of Tennessee. The units in question would be two divisions of the First Corps, commanded by Longstreet.[22]

Davis also offered Lee the overall command of the forthcoming offensive. The latter did not decline, although his written reply revealed little enthusiasm for the scheme.[23] Nevertheless, for days rumors swept Richmond that Lee was going west, perhaps with a corps, perhaps with his whole army.[24] But Davis, aware that Lee was less than eager to leave Virginia, and concerned about the morale of the understrength and outnumbered Army of Northern Virginia should its commander depart, ultimately decided to leave Lee in command in the East and Bragg in charge of the Army of Tennessee.[25]

Lee returned to his headquarters at Orange Court House, Virginia. The strength of his army stood at about fifty-six thousand men (August 31), down from sixty-eight thousand three weeks before (August 10).[26] The departure of Longstreet's corps would strip another fourteen thousand from the army's rolls.[27] Meade's army totaled about eighty-nine thousand (August 31); thus, Lee was outnumbered by better than two to one.[28] Lee, of course, did not know the exact strength of the Army of the Potomac, but he knew that his army was heavily outnumbered by Meade's and expected the latter to make the most of the situation.[29] Lee, expecting an attack, warned Davis and Seddon that they ought to begin work on the defenses of Richmond. But the offensive-minded commander of the Army of Northern Virginia also noted that if he were only "a little stronger" he would undertake a preemptive strike against Meade that would forestall the Union offensive, which Lee feared would force the army "back to Richmond."[30]

As Lee warily watched Meade, the divisions of Major Generals John Bell Hood and Lafayette McLaws, along with other units detached from the Army of Northern Virginia, began their trek west. On September 19 and 20, Longstreet's troops joined with Bragg's on the field of Chickamauga and played a major role in winning the battle. The beaten Federals streamed back toward Chattanooga, barely holding on to the important rail junction.

Reports of the major Union defeat spread throughout the Confederacy. Davis wrote Lee on September 21, heralding the victory, expressing a hope that the pursuit would render it "complete," stating his decision to go to the West as soon as possible, and regretting that "want of an adequate force" prevented Lee from availing himself "of the opportunity afforded by the present condition of the enemy."[31] But Lee remained in a defensive mind-set, writing on September 27 that he believed that Meade would soon strike south with "overwhelming numbers."[32]

Only on September 28, when Lee received the first reports about detachments from Meade's army reinforcing the Army of the Cumberland, did the commander of the Army of Northern Virginia stop sending pessimistic appraisals of his situation to Richmond. Lee's less foreboding reports, combined with the news from the West, brought a sense of relief to the Confederate capital. To those familiar with Lee's earlier correspondence, it appeared that Bragg's triumph in the West had not only halted the Federal advance, but also had saved the Army of Northern Virginia from being forced back to the gates of the capital.[33] On October 1, clerk Jones noted in his diary: "Bragg's victory has given us a respite in the East, and soon the bad roads will put an end to the maneuvering of armies until next year. I doubt whether the Yankees will desire another campaign in Virginia."[34]

JONES'S CONCLUSION that the campaigning season had ended in the East was mistaken. He noted in his diary the next day: "It is now said that Gen. Lee, despairing of being attacked in his chosen position, has resolved to attack Meade." The word in the capital was that Lee was planning an offensive of his own that might lead his army back across the Potomac, perhaps into Pennsylvania to threaten the state capital at Harrisburg![35] Were the rumors true? And if so, what had prompted Lee to resume the offensive?

Lee had decided to attack Meade, although there is little evidence that he ever entertained prospects of returning to Pennsylvania so late in the year.[36] That word of Lee's intention to strike north had filtered back to Richmond by October 2 indicates that the commander of the Army of Northern Virginia must have decided to go over to the offensive almost as soon as he learned that the Federal high command was shifting two of Meade's corps—the Eleventh and the Twelfth—west to check the Confederate advance in Tennessee.[37]

But why an offensive? From Lee's official correspondence, it is unclear whether he sought to keep Meade busy to prevent further detachments from being sent west, to drive Meade out of Virginia, or to bring on a battle. During the campaign, Lee offered several reasons for his move north, although he never mentioned engaging Meade's army until *after* the battle of Bristoe Station on October 14. On the ninth, with his army on the march, Lee penned a short note to the Confederate commander in the Shenandoah Valley, Brigadier General John D. Imboden, noting: "It is a matter of great importance, in my judgment, that our troops should advance upon the enemy in all quarters, for the purpose of preventing him from re-enforcing points more seriously threatened, if nothing more can be accomplished."[38] On the thirteenth, Lee wrote Secretary Seddon that the army was on the move "with the view of throwing [Meade] farther back toward Washington."[39] Not until two days later, after the debacle at Bristoe Station, did Lee inform the secretary of war that the Army of Northern Virginia had maneuvered "with the view of turning the right flank of the enemy and intercepting his line of retreat."[40] In an October 17 letter to President Davis, as the Army of Northern Virginia retreated back toward the Rappahannock, Lee wrote that he had moved north "with the view of bringing on an engagement with the army of General Meade."[41] And on the twenty-third, in an interim report on the campaign to the adjutant and inspector general, General Samuel Cooper, Lee stated for the record that he had moved north "with the design of bringing on an engagement with the Federal army."[42]

The memoirs of officers serving with the Army of Northern Virginia support the view that Lee moved north with the expectation, or at least the hope, that he would be able to engage the Army of the Potomac to advantage. Walter H. Taylor wrote that Lee marched north "with a view of reaching [Meade's] flank or forcing him to retire."[43] Early, who was with Lee, Hill (Third Corps), and Ewell (Second Corps) when they met on Clark's Mountain on October 3 to survey the ground on the right of Meade's army, wrote that "General Lee determined to move around Meade's right flank and attack him."[44]

Nevertheless, given the somewhat conflicting documentary record, historians have had difficulty determining why Lee moved north. Suggested motives for Lee's offensive fall into three general categories: to gain space, to gain time, or to gain a battlefield victory. William Hassler, in his biography of A. P. Hill, suggested that Lee crossed the Rapidan to force Meade back and to clear Virginia of Federal troops.[45] James D. McCabe Jr., in his study of Lee, wrote that he sought to weaken Meade or, at the minimum, to forestall an advance by the Army of the Potomac until it would be too late in the year to move on Richmond.[46] Shelby Foote, in his narrative of the Civil War, stated that Lee, aware that the detachment of two Union corps had reduced the odds against him from two to one to eight to five, struck north hoping to initiate a replay of the campaign of Second Manassas.[47] James I. Robertson, in his biography of A. P. Hill, wrote that Meade's loss of two corps "brought the opposing armies almost to numerical equality—whereupon Lee again determined to take the offensive."[48] Emory M. Thomas, while noting that the Army of Northern Virginia was still heavily "outnumbered," wrote that the ever-aggressive Lee "hoped to interpose his army between Meade and Washington and compel his enemy to give battle in the open."[49] Lee's principal biographer, Douglas Southall Freeman, offered a composite view, suggesting several reasons for Lee's offensive: to prevent further Union detachments; to force Meade north of the Potomac to spare northern Virginia further "distresses" related to a winter occupation; to safeguard Confederate railroads from Union cavalry raiders; and to gain maneuvering ground for the 1864 campaign.[50]

There is no documentary evidence to support the idea that Lee moved north to gain ground. As Longstreet noted in his letters to Lee in early September, there was no point in having the Army of Northern Virginia move north toward Washington since it lacked the strength to cross the Potomac, assault the city's southern defenses, or to maintain itself south of the river. The northern counties of Virginia along Lee's intended line of march had been stripped bare and left uncultivated, and could not sustain an army that would have to live off the land for several weeks. Lee admitted as much in an October 15 letter to Seddon, writing: "It is impossible for us to remain where we are, as the country is destitute of provisions for men and animals, and the railroad bridges on this side of the Rappahannock (and I learn at the river) have been destroyed."[51] Lee had the option to move west, into Loudon County, but such a maneuver would uncover the direct route from Washington to Richmond.[52] Moreover, Lee had been over the ground only three months before during his retreat from Gettysburg, knew the state of the counties in question, and knew also that there was no position between the Rapidan and Washington that he considered good defensive ground. He had written on August 4: "I could find no field in Culpeper offering advantages for battle, and any taken could be so easily avoided should the enemy wish to reach the south bank of the Rapidan, that I thought it advisable at once to retire to that bank."[53]

If there was little to be gained in maneuvering Meade out of his position along the Rapidan, what of the prospects of battle? At the time of Lee's discussions with Davis in Richmond in late August–early September, the Army of Northern Virginia had a strength of about fifty-six thousand, while Meade's army totaled about eighty-nine thousand men. The odds against Lee were about 1.58 to 1—not ideal for an offensive, but better than they would be over the coming months. In late September, before the detachment of the Eleventh and the Twelfth Corps, Meade's army topped one hundred thousand, while Lee's, following the detachment of Longstreet, dropped to about forty-four thousand. The odds then stood at 2.29 to 1, and Lee viewed Meade's army as an immense horde about to sweep south toward Richmond. The transfer west of the Eleventh and the Twelfth Corps did improve the odds, as Foote and Robertson suggested, but not by much. Because of the continued reinforcement of units weakened at Gettysburg, at the end of September Meade still commanded eighty-nine thousand men, despite the detachment of the two corps.[54] The odds stood at 2.02 to 1.[55]

Lee, of course, did not have access to the muster rolls of Meade's army. And there were reports from scouts and agents that the Army of the Potomac was weaker than it actually was. Reports reached Lee that indicated two additional Federal corps had also been sent west.[56] Jeb Stuart forwarded a report on October 6 that stated that Meade's army was "very much demoralized."[57] War Department clerk Jones wrote in his diary that Major General Arnold Elzey, who commanded the garrison force in the capital, was telling everyone in Richmond that Meade's army had shrunk to a force of between thirty thousand and fifty thousand![58]

But there is no evidence that such grossly inaccurate speculation had any impact on Lee's decision to move north. He dismissed reports that more than two corps had been sent west, or that the Eleventh and the Twelfth Corps mustered between twenty and twenty-five thousand men. He believed that the two formations together probably controlled no more than twelve thousand men, and noted in a letter to Davis: "They are considered two of the smallest and indifferent corps."[59] Without a doubt, when Lee moved north, he knew that Meade's Army of the Potomac was much larger than the Army of Northern Virginia.

In letters to the president and secretary of war written after Bristoe Station, Lee did suggest that his abortive offensive might have gained him some time.[60] But it is clear from his correspondence that this was but a serendipitous by-product, rather than an anticipated objective of the march north. As Lee wrote Seddon on October 15: "Though the enemy has suffered less than I wished, some good may yet result from the fact of his being compelled to fall back before us."[61] Moreover, given the heavy odds against the Confederates, it is ludicrous to suggest that Lee, assuming his intentions were primarily defensive and meant to gain time, was better off fighting Meade on the move near Bull Run than entrenched south of the Rapidan. Meade was prepared, although somewhat reluctantly, to attack before the campaigning season ended, as he demonstrated at Mine Run in November. But Lee was a master of defensive warfare, even when heavily outnumbered, as he had shown at Fredericksburg in 1862 and Chancellorsville in 1863, and would demonstrate to Grant in the spring and summer of 1864. Lee did not have to take the offensive in the fall of 1863 to prevent George Gordon Meade from driving to Richmond before the onset of winter.

Nor was Lee's heavily outnumbered army, or its commander, well prepared for a fall offensive.[62] Lee's health was poor. He was suffering from back pains that left him unable to sit on a horse, as well as the continued symptoms of the heart trouble that would ultimately kill him.[63] The command structure of the army had not been reformed since Gettysburg, where neither Ewell nor Hill had shone particularly brightly as corps commanders.[64] Lee's ablest surviving subordinate—Longstreet—was in the West. The units of the Army of Northern Virginia were understrength, undersupplied, and unpaid, and the horses were in poor shape.[65] Lee later blamed the poor condition of the army and the lateness of the season for his abrupt end to the campaign. He wrote Seddon on October 19: "Nothing prevented my continuing in his front but the destitute condition of the men, thousands of whom are barefooted, a greater number partially shod, and nearly all without blankets, or warm clothing."[66] But the men were "barefooted," and the season late, when Lee sent the army across the Rapidan on October 9.

It is easy to blame Quartermaster General Lawton for the failure to supply the army adequately for an offensive, as did Freeman who wrote: "The quartermaster's corps had not issued enough shoes before the advance."[67] In an October 12 letter, Lawton acknowledged as much, noting Lee's "recent" requests "for shoes for men and horses, and blankets for the former."[68] But resources were tight in the blockaded Confederacy. Lawton was already busy supplying an offensive in the West and was scraping the proverbial bottom of the barrel to keep the armies of the Confederacy in the field. Nor did Lee's penchant for hastily planned, unannounced offensives allow Lawton *any* advance warning that the Army of Northern Virginia was about to strike north.

Why such secrecy about the army's movements? Freeman attributed Lee's silence about the coming offensive to a desire to shield his plan of operations from the enemy.[69] "Insistence upon secrecy was typical of Lee," Coddington wrote; "he was extremely reticent about revealing his plans to anyone except the Secretary of War, the President, and now and then a few of his intimates in the army such as Lieutenant General James Longstreet or certain members of his staff."[70] There were few actual military "secrets" during the Civil War, a fact that much annoyed Lee. He knew, for example, that the plans for the movement of Longstreet's troops to Tennessee became known in Washington not long after Davis decided to reinforce Bragg. As early as September 6, Washington was abuzz with reports that detachments from Lee's army were on their way west, and on September 14 Meade confirmed that Longstreet's corps was no longer with Lee.[71]

But Lee, as he had demonstrated before the Maryland and Gettysburg campaigns, was as determined to keep information concerning his movements secret from his civilian masters in Richmond as he was about keeping them secret from the Federals. Robert Garlick Hill Kean, the head of the Confederate Bureau of War, wrote of Lee after Gettysburg: "He is as silent as the grave, has become nearly as costive as Johnston. When he deigns to make a communication of any importance it is in a letter to the President, or telegram—always brief and jejeune. Beauregard is the only general who keeps the Department advised *fully* of affairs in his department, of his plans and prospects."[72] As a result, Davis and Seddon had no reason to suspect, until rumors began to circulate in the capital, that Lee was about to launch another offensive. No word of preparations or planning is evident in the extant correspondence. In an October 5 letter to the president, Lee made no mention of moving north. In fact, he suggested that Davis go to Tennessee to straighten out command problems in the West. "I think if Your Excellency could make it convenient to visit that country," Lee wrote, "you would be able to reconcile many difficulties and unite the scattered troops."[73] Only on October 9, when the offensive was already under way, did Lee inform his neighbors in the Shenandoah Valley and western Virginia that the main army was on the march, and suggest supporting offensives in those sectors.[74] Not until Seddon received an October 10 letter from Lee did the secretary of war have any indication that the Army of Northern Virginia might have gone over to the offensive. In a rather cryptic communication, Lee wrote that he had indications, which he discounted, that Meade was about to strike, but then noted in passing that Stuart's cavalry had engaged Federal troopers near James City.[75] Seddon, no doubt, realized that James City was north, not south, of the Rapidan. The next day, Lee penned another letter to the secretary of war:

> Yesterday I moved the army into this position with the hope of getting an opportunity to strike a blow at the enemy. I regretted to hear that it was announced in one of the Richmond

papers of yesterday that this army was in motion and had crossed the Rapidan. All such publications are injurious to us. We have difficulties enough to overcome interposed by our enemies without having them augmented by our friends. I wish I could impress upon the editors the importance of rejecting from their papers all mention of military movements until the result has been obtained. *The announcement was erroneous*, but still the information received by the enemy would serve to place him upon his guard.[76]

Lee, despite this bold denial, was already over the Rapidan, as he admitted in an October 23 report: "This army crossed that river [the Rapidan] on the 9th instant."[77]And if Seddon looked closely at the October 11 letter, it bore at the top (perhaps the result of clerical oversight since for the past two days, while Lee was on the move, no location had been given for the army's headquarters in correspondence), the dateline "Madison Court House," which anyone familiar with the eastern theater knew was, like James City, north of the Rapidan River.[78]

Why the charade? As Freeman admitted: "The appearance of Federal cavalry in front of Stuart . . . [on October 10] showed that the Confederate movement had been discovered and that Lee could not hope to catch Meade off his guard."[79] Yet the next day Lee lied about the location of the army in a letter to the secretary of war. As events would demonstrate, Meade was far better informed about Lee's movements than was Seddon. Not until October 16 did Seddon know enough about Lee's already failed offensive to write Davis, who was by then in the West.[80]

Lee was determined to keep his civilian superiors in the dark about his operations because he feared that they might direct him to forego such a potentially dangerous move concurrent with Bragg's offensive in the West. Immediately after the battle of Chickamauga, Davis did lament the fact that Lee was not strong enough to take full advantage of the situation, but during the interim the president had done nothing to remedy those circumstances. Lee did not regard the transfer west of the "indifferent" Eleventh and Twelfth Corps so great a loss to the Federal army that he might have suddenly considered some window of opportunity now open for a decisive Confederate counterstroke. Nor did Lee act as one might expect a commander of a bedraggled army to have acted, and as Lee had acted himself before the start of the Gettysburg campaign—by attempting to use his forthcoming offensive as leverage to extract basic supplies such as shoes, overcoats, and blankets from the quartermaster before undertaking a fall march around Meade's right flank.

Lee moved north to engage Meade because the latter had not come south. In Lee's mind, Meade's cautious inactivity permitted the politicians back in Richmond to consider it safe to detach troops from the entrenched Army of Northern Virginia. Had Meade been more aggressive in August, or Lee been able to take the offensive, Davis would never have sent Longstreet west. Lee knew that Davis and Seddon had begun to view the Army of Northern Virginia as a potential source of reinforcements for other hard-pressed theaters. The crisis along the coast, especially at Charleston and Wilmington, was growing acute, at least in the eyes of the local commanders. Throughout September Major General W. H. C. Whiting, commander of the Department of North Carolina, and Governor Zebulon Vance of North Carolina sent almost daily requests for reinforcements to Davis and Seddon.[81] Lee, who had been in Richmond earlier in the month, was well aware of this.[82] And he knew that not all of the First Corps troops lost in early September went with Longstreet to the West. Some headed to Charleston. Pickett's Division went to the Richmond defenses, thus freeing other brigades to join Whiting in North Carolina. In fact, on the day before Lee began his offensive, Adjutant and Inspector General Cooper directed that the Seventh Confederate Cavalry Regiment, a unit of North Carolina troopers earmarked for service with Lee, remain instead in state because of the looming crisis along the coast.[83] Lee knew that if both he and Meade remained inactive, the Army of Northern Virginia would come under increasing pressure to transfer additional units to more active fronts. The only way to prevent such detachments was for the Army of Northern Virginia to undertake an offensive. That Lee believed he would have to detach additional units from his army if it were not engaged is evident in his letter to Secretary of War Seddon on October 19, after the check at Bristoe Station. "If you can give me any exact information as to the numbers and position of the enemy at any point where you think it most expedient to send the troops," Lee wrote, "I shall be very glad to meet your views."[84]

Lee swung his army around Meade's flank primarily to frustrate any scheme hatched in Richmond to detach additional troops. He hoped that during the course of operations the commander of the Army of the Potomac would make a mistake that would allow Lee to win a victory significant enough to justify the effort. Lee knew his offensive would gain him neither time nor space. He knew that he could not keep his army in the field north of the Rappahannock. Also, given Meade's innate sense of caution, the strong defensive position occupied by the Army of Northern Virginia along the Rapidan River, and the lateness of the season, Lee realized that there was no need to preempt a Federal offensive. And at this stage of the war could Lee have held no illusions that his army of forty-four thousand "barefooted" men could somehow engage and destroy a force more than twice its own size. Nor was the operation without risk for the Army of Northern Virginia, as events would demonstrate. Lee's willingness to chance an offensive was based not on a sound assessment of the military situation, but on a hope, or expectation, of his adversary's incompetence. As Lee wrote on October 9 to Major General Samuel Jones, commander of the Department of Western Virginia: "I think it very important that our troops everywhere should advance upon the enemy, even if nothing else can be accomplished excepting preventing him from reinforcing points now threatened. *Of course, if opportunity offers to do more, it should be made use of.*"[85]

Lee, as he had in the Maryland and Gettysburg campaigns, was sending his army north without a fully developed plan of operations but with a conviction that his opponent would falter and provide the Army of Northern Virginia with an opportunity to strike a blow. But assumptions about the incompetence of one's opponent are not the basis for sound strategic planning. Nor did Lee have any reason to suspect that Meade, who had handled his army cautiously but ably since taking over in June, would stumble. As the Gettysburg campaign demonstrated, while Meade was cautious, he was no bungler. The chief bunglers at Gettysburg had been Lee's own lieutenants.

WHILE LEE'S MOVES may have surprised Seddon, they had not fooled Meade. Days before official word of the Confederate offensive reached Richmond, Meade was aware of Lee's preparations. As early as October 2, Federal commanders picked up the first hints of unusual activity.[86] On October 3, Lee, Hill, Ewell, and Jubal Early held a council of war on Clark's Mountain, where eavesdropping Confederate signalmen overheard Lee announce his decision to attack.[87] Across the river, Union signalmen were also listening in, and intercepting messages regarding the unusual presence of the senior commanders of the Army of Northern Virginia.[88] Later that same day, Meade telegraphed Washington that he expected Lee to commence a movement of some kind.[89]

While Lee's reports, during and after the campaign, noted that the offensive commenced on October 9, preliminary moves actually began on the eighth.[90] At 11:00 A.M. on October 8, Major General Andrew A. Humphreys, Meade's chief of staff, alerted Major General John Sedgwick, commander of the Federal Sixth Corps, that Lee was marching around the army's right. Meade had already ordered several countermoves.[91]

The excellent work of Meade's signalmen on Cedar Mountain affords a good view not only of Federal vigilance, but also of the jury-rigged nature of Lee's offensive. On October 3, the Yankee signal station intercepted the following messages passed between two of Stuart's cavalry units—Question: "When do you expect the men's rations?" Reply: "God only knows."[92] On October 7, only twenty-four hours before Lee's offensive began, Union signalmen intercepted a belated message from Lee to Stuart: "Send me some good guides for country between Madison Court-House and Woodville."[93]

Nevertheless, Meade was unsure as to just what Lee had in mind. Was he planning a short enfilading hook against the army's right flank? Or yet another sweeping march that would carry the Army of Northern Virginia deep into the rear of the Army of the Potomac? To find out, Meade pushed his cavalry westward in an effort to penetrate Stuart's cavalry screen. In the meantime, the Federal commander, with rivers to his front and rear, and concerned about his line of communications stretching back along the Orange & Alexandria Railroad to Washington, ordered the Army of the Potomac to cross over to the north bank of the Rappahannock.[94]

As these movements were in progress, reports from Meade's cavalry convinced him that Lee was concentrating his army around Culpeper. Meade ordered several corps to recross the Rappahannock and to concentrate on Culpeper, where he expected to engage Lee's army.[95]

Unfortunately for Meade, the reports from his cavalry were inaccurate. Later intelligence indicated that Lee had himself crossed the Rappahannock and was already in the Army of the Potomac's rear. Late on the evening of October 12, Meade's staff issued new orders that sent the army hustling north in an effort to beat Lee to Centreville.[96]

Lee was now around Meade's flank, with the Army of Northern Virginia marching in two main columns along the Culpeper-Warrenton-Centreville axis. Troops from Ewell's Second Corps formed the eastern, or inside column, while the men from Hill's Third Corps formed the western, or outside, column.[97]

As Lee's troopers and infantrymen raced north, their morale rose. Twice before the fields near Manassas had witnessed Confederate victories. And now, the Yankees were on the run again, with the Rebels in hot pursuit. Captain James A. Graham of Pitt County's Marlboro Guards—Company G of the Twenty-seventh North Carolina—later wrote: "Guns, knapsacks, blankets, etc., strewn along the road showed that the enemy was moving in rapid retreat, and prisoners sent in every few minutes confirmed our opinion that they were fleeing in haste. It was almost like boys chasing a hare."[98] Both Shelby Foote and Douglas Southall Freeman note that the spirit of Manassas filled the army with a sense of expectation—an expectation of victory.[99]

But as the army marched north, Lee's campaign once again became derailed. Eager to make the most of the fighting power of his outnumbered infantry, Lee had entrusted the duty of rear guard to his nephew Fitzhugh Lee's division of cavalry in what was now termed Stuart's cavalry corps. Despite the difficulties that had developed because of a lack of cavalry leading the advances into Maryland and Pennsylvania, Lee posted his remaining cavalry on his right, and not on the left or leading flank of the army as it looped to the west and north. As Stuart wrote in his report:

> In compliance with the instructions of the commanding general, Maj. Gen. Fitzhugh Lee was left with his division, supported by two brigades of infantry, on the line of the Rapidan to observe the enemy in that direction, while I proceeded in personal command of [Major General Wade] Hampton's division—that officer being still detained from duty by wounds received at Gettysburg—to guard the right flank of the Army of Northern Virginia in its advance by way of Madison Court House in the execution of a flank movement on the enemy then in Culpeper.[100]

On October 13, Lee concentrated his army around Warrenton: Hill on the left, Ewell in the center, and Stuart with Hampton's division on the right. The Confederates were facing to the north and east, while the Federals were retreating toward the northeast along the tracks of the Orange & Alexandria Railroad. About ten o'clock in the morning, as Hill's and Ewell's infantry rested, Lee directed Stuart to conduct a reconnaissance toward Catlett's Station, east and a bit south of Warrenton. During the course of that movement, Stuart stumbled into what he later termed an "embarrassing situation." Stuart was trapped between two columns of retreating Federal troops—one moving through Auburn, about six miles east and a little south of Warrenton, and the other along the railroad. Burke Davis, in his popular biography of Stuart, wrote that he had taken "his men into a trap which provided laughter for the army for months."[101]

Indeed, some of the anecdotes from that night, when the Rebel cavalry lay so close to the Yankees that they could overhear their conversations, were humorous. But the situation was deadly serious, and Stuart knew it. He sent messengers carrying dispatches asking for assistance, and recommended that an attack would strike the retreating Federals in the flank. What Stuart did not understand was that he had set in motion a chain of events that would lead to disaster the following day.

One of Stuart's calls for assistance reached Ewell at his headquarters near Warrenton at 4:00 A.M. on the fourteenth. According to the Second Corps diary of the campaign, Ewell immediately "moved Rodes, Early, & Johnson to [Stuart's] help."[102] As the Rebels approached, the Federals in the westernmost column, already intent on withdrawal, suddenly and unexpectedly found themselves caught between the two fires of Ewell's infantry and Stuart's cavalry and hastened their retreat. Early then resumed the advance on Ewell's left, with Rodes in the center and Johnson on the right. Unfortunately for Ewell, the effort to rescue Stuart—deploying the regiments from column into line and sending them off the roads and cross-country—led to a four-hour delay in the planned advance to the Orange & Alexandria Railroad and thence to Bristoe Station.[103]

As Ewell moved cross-country to support Stuart, Powell Hill's men set out on a predawn flank march. Hill wrote:

> On the morning of the 14th instant I left my camp, 1 mile dis-
> tant from Warrenton, on the Amissville turnpike, at 5 A.M., and
> in obedience to orders from the general commanding took the
> Warrenton and Alexandria turnpike until reaching Broad Run
> Church, then took the road by Greenwich and on to Bristoe
> Station, the division of Major-General [Richard H.] Anderson
> leading.[104]

Shortly after Anderson reached the cutoff for the road that led
through Greenwich to Bristoe, Hill received reports that there
were Federal troops to the north. He directed Anderson to continue along the turnpike toward Buckland Mills, while Major
General Cadmus Wilcox's and Harry Heth's divisions turned
east and followed the road through Greenwich toward Bristoe.
As a result of Anderson's march, Hill, according to his campaign
report, "found the force referred to to be of cavalry, that it had
already disappeared, and that Maj. Gen. Fitz. Lee had come up
with his cavalry on my left flank."

Fitz Lee, whose division had formed the rear guard, had
caught up with the rest of the army near Warrenton on the thirteenth. At last, Uncle Robert would have some cavalry to cover
the advance of his left. According to Fitz Lee's report: "On the
14th, I was ordered to move on the left flank of our army, and
marched via New Baltimore and Gainesville to the vicinity of
Bristoe Station, where I remained all night."[105]

But the road that passes through New Baltimore and Gainesville—the Warrenton Turnpike—does not lead to Bristoe, but to
Manassas. Nor is there any evidence that Fitz Lee's troopers
came anywhere near Bristoe Station, despite their commander's
claim that he spent the night there. In fact, John R. Chambliss
Jr., the colonel of the Thirteenth Virginia Cavalry and the man
who led Fitz Lee's own brigade while he acted as division commander, wrote that on October 14 "the brigade moved with division" toward Manassas.[106]

There are several possible explanations for this discrepancy.
First, Lee, or someone on his staff, could have given Fitz Lee
poor directions, although this seems unlikely since the route

laid out in Hill's orders was accurate. Second, Fitz Lee could have missed the fork for the road to Greenwich and Bristoe—although if he had, Anderson, who met him along the turnpike near Buckland Mills, would certainly have so informed the army commander's nephew of his mistake. Just east of Buckland Mills there was another road that led to Greenwich. Fitz Lee could have moved on from there to Bristoe. Third, Lee might have actually ordered his nephew to move toward Manassas. But then why would Fitz Lee later claim that he had been "ordered" to Bristoe, and lie about his presence there? The fourth, and most likely, explanation is that Fitz Lee decided to move toward Manassas, instead of Bristoe, on his own initiative. Fitz Lee's cavalry had only reached Warrenton on the afternoon of October 13, and had become involved in the skirmishing near Auburn that led to Stuart's, though not Fitz Lee's, entrapment. The Third Corps had bivouacked northeast of Warrenton along the turnpike. Given Hill's location and early 5:00 A.M. start, Fitz Lee probably found his troopers moving slowly along the road behind the infantry of the Third Corps. Rather than continue to follow Hill's slow moving infantry, or advancing cross-country in an effort to get out ahead of the Third Corps when Hill's divisions took the right fork to Greenwich, Fitz Lee decided to continue along the turnpike, where he ran into the rear of Anderson's division near Buckland Mills. Since Anderson, as per Hill's orders, intended to move south along the road that led from Buckland to Greenwich, Fitz Lee remained on the now wide open turnpike and continued his march in the direction of Gainesville and thence toward Manassas, where he might intercept the fleeing Federal columns on a field that twice before had blessed the Confederacy with a splendid victory. Whatever the actual reason for Fitz Lee's movements on October 14, the fact remains that he did not advance, despite apparent orders to do so, toward Bristoe.

As a result, Powell Hill's infantrymen were advancing, as they had on the morning of July 1, 1863, without the benefit of cavalry probing ahead. Initially, everything seemed to be going along well. In the afternoon, with Harry Heth's division in the lead, the Rebels were hard on the heels of the retreating Federals, 150 of whom Heth's men picked up as "stragglers." From the prisoners, Hill learned that he was pursuing the Federal Third Corps.[107]

When Hill reached the high ground overlooking Broad Run he could see the Yankees on the other side, some resting, others resuming their march toward Manassas. "I determined that no time must be lost," Hill later reported, "and hurried up Heth's division, forming it in line of battle along the crest of the hills and parallel to Broad Run." Hill directed Major W. T. Poague's artillery battalion to "open on the enemy" as Heth's men advanced on a two-brigade front—Colonel W. W. Kirkland's and Brigadier General John Rogers Cooke's North Carolinians, with Brigadier General W. S. Walker's Virginia-Alabama brigade in the rear. The Confederate fire had the desired effect. Hill noted that the Federals "were evidently taken completely by surprise, and retired in the utmost confusion." Hill, sensing an opportunity, ordered Heth to advance by his left to the run, to cross at the ford, "and to press the enemy."

As Heth began the movement, what had seemed to be a moment of impending Confederate victory turned into a nightmare. Federal troops suddenly materialized on Heth's right flank. In his report, Hill termed these men "skirmishers," while Heth wrote of "a heavy column of the enemy."[108] As to exactly what happened next, the contemporary record is unclear.

According to Hill's account, he directed Cooke's brigade to cover the flank of the advance. Cooke's men changed front and quickly drove off the skirmishers. Hill then ordered up Anderson's division to cover the right flank of Heth's advance.

But Heth, alerted by Cooke to the Yankee presence on the flank, later wrote that he reported the presence of the Union troops to Hill, who hesitated and "deferred" the movement for about ten minutes. Only then did he decide to send the troops forward. The corps commander assured Heth that Dick Anderson's men would cover the flank of the advancing line and sent a courier to Cooke bearing orders to "advance *at once*."[109] "Well," Cooke replied, "I will advance and if they flank me, I will face my men about and cut my way out." Cooke turned to his regiment and gave the command, "Forward!"[110]

Unbeknownst to Hill and Heth, elements of another Federal corps—Major General Gouverneur K. Warren's Second—were deployed on their right, hidden behind a high railroad embankment that carried the Orange & Alexandria Railroad across the run. Warren had arrived "as cannonading had begun," and witnessed the Confederate line going forward toward Broad Run. The quick-thinking Warren, who had saved Meade at Little Round Top on the second day at Gettysburg, ordered his artillery into action, skirmishers deployed, and a line formed to hold the embankment and some rifle pits near the crossing. He later wrote: "A more inspiring scene could not be imagined. The enemy's line of battle boldly moving forward, one part of our own steadily awaiting it and another moving against it at the double-quick, while the artillery was taking up position at a gallop and going into action."[111]

The splendor of the moment also struck Hill, who wrote: "The three brigades (Cooke's, Kirkland's, and Walker's) advanced in beautiful order and quite steadily." Unfortunately for the men of Heth's division, the advance ran into "an exceedingly strong" position, heavy musketry, and enfilading artillery fire. The men nevertheless moved forward, "gained the railroad, clearing it for a time of the enemy." But both brigadiers—Cooke and Kirkland—fell and their men found themselves under heavy fire. They could not possibly hold their position and were forced back, according to Hill, "in good order."[112]

The battle looked somewhat different to Colonel Edward D. Hall, commander of the Forty-sixth North Carolina Infantry, who took charge of the brigade when Cooke went down.[113] At that moment, heavy musketry had halted the forward movement of the brigade about two hundred yards from the railroad embankment. "I soon saw that a rapid advance must be made or a withdrawal," Hall noted. "I chose the former." When the advance resumed, as a young lieutenant with the Fifteenth North Carolina would later write, the North Carolinians "were subjected to such a terrific fire from the enemy that their lines were mowed down like grain before a reaper."[114] Another wrote: "It was the hottest place I ever saw. Sharpsburg was not near so hot. The engagement commenced about three o'clock and lasted till near night and in that time we lost fully two thirds of our Reg't."[115] Hall's men charged to within forty yards of the embankment, but there the men's morale yielded to common sense. Some regiments fell back in good order; some did not.

The men of the Eleventh North Carolina actually made it to the railroad and drove the Federals from their positions near Broad Run. But both the regiment's flanks were exposed; no additional troops moved up in support. There was obviously nothing to be done other than to retreat. Unfortunately, as the regiment's historian noted, "a number of the men shrank from [re]crossing the open field" and surrendered.[116]

In a matter of minutes, Heth's division lost 1,361 men, about 20 percent of its strength. One regiment, the Twenty-seventh North Carolina, lost 290 of its 416 men, including 33 of 36 officers.[117] A participant later noted: "The battle only lasted about forty minutes of actual fighting, and I doubt if such carnage was ever known in the same length of time."[118]

Hill canceled the advance and waited for the rest of his own and Ewell's corps to reach the field.[119] But it was nearly dusk before the Second Corps, its advance delayed by the need to rescue Stuart, arrived. Nevertheless, Ewell ordered Early's division to advance on Hill's right. Ewell's diary of the campaign noted that Early promptly pushed John Brown Gordon's brigade "ahead," but that Hill had in the meantime "stopped fighting."[120] Despite some continued skirmishing and artillery exchanges, the opportunity for battle quickly disappeared. That evening, Warren's men crossed Broad Run and continued their march toward Centreville.

The next day, Lee and Hill toured the battlefield, and the commander of the Third Corps explained—or attempted to explain—what had happened. Lee listened patiently, then turned to Hill and said: "Well, well, General, bury these poor men and let us say no more about it."[121]

Hill's compulsion to assault the retreating Federals ought not to come as a surprise. The immediate responsibility for the fiasco at Bristoe was, of course, his. He attacked without proper reconnaissance. He disregarded warnings from experienced subordinates—including Cooke, who was in the firing line. But Hill obviously believed that he was acting in concert with his commander's concept for the campaign. What exactly had passed between Hill and Lee during the march north, and during the predawn hours of October 14, is not known. But from the early start of the march on the fourteenth, and Hill's obvious aggressiveness, one might well surmise that his purpose that day was to catch up with and to engage the Federal rear guard before it escaped across Broad Run and effectively brought Lee's offensive to an end. Hill's aggressiveness mirrors Lee's own willingness to take on an army twice the size of his own. Or, as Fitzhugh Lee later wrote of his uncle's theory of war: "In planning all dangers should be seen, in execution none, unless very formidable."[122]

Once again, one of the Army of Northern Virginia's offensives had miscarried; once again, one of Lee's corps commanders had failed. Dick Ewell had been too slow to attack at Cemetery Hill, Powell Hill too quick to press the assault at Bristoe Station.[123] Despite the fact that Lee's army held the field, he knew that he had failed and had to retreat south. In an October 23 report, he noted matter of factly that Hill's attack had been "repulsed with some loss, and five pieces of artillery, with a number of prisoners, captured."[124] Hill reported: "In conclusion, I am convinced that I made the attack too hastily, and at the same time that a delay of half an hour, and there would have been no enemy to attack. In that event I believe I should equally have blamed myself for not attacking at once."[125]

ON OCTOBER 14, Lee's decentralized approach to command had failed to operate with its usual, or at least expected, efficiency. A system that had worked so well, so often, came untracked, just as it had during the Gettysburg campaign. In part, the problem was one of personnel—the need for experienced and capable corps commanders, men such as Longstreet and Jackson. Lee supposedly once said of Jackson: "I have but to show him my design, and I know that if it can be done it will be done. No need for me to send or watch him. Straight as the needle to the pole he advances to the execution of my purpose."[126] But, unfortunately for Lee, Jackson was dead in the fall of 1863. Even Longstreet was gone, off with his corps in Tennessee. Ewell had not displayed comparable drive and initiative at Gettysburg. And now Hill, at Bristoe, demonstrated that he, too, could not handle a corps.[127]

There were many men in the Army of Northern Virginia, officers and soldiers alike, who blamed Heth for the debacle at Bristoe Station. Walter Taylor wrote: "It was a shameful affair and whilst I am unable to say *who* was responsible I regret that nearly every one who dares speak openly blames our friend Genl. H[eth] (your cousin's husband)."[128] But others considered Hill the culprit. A soldier with the Twenty-seventh North Carolina wrote his sister: "It is the general impression out of the army that Gen. Heath [*sic*] is to blame but I think A. P. Hill is the man that made the mistake and the blame should rest upon him."[129]

But Lee must also bear some of the responsibility for the failures of his subordinates. Once again, he used his cavalry as rear guard and led the advance northward with his infantry. When Fitz Lee caught up with the army at Warrenton, Lee employed his nephew's division on the left flank but it failed, for whatever reason, to scout ahead of Hill's advance on October 14. While no one can say whether Uncle Robert or Nephew Fitz was at fault, neither Powell Hill nor Harry Heth were responsible for the absence of cavalry on the road to Bristoe Station.

Taylor, no doubt reflecting the view of the headquarters staff of the Army of Northern Virginia, and perhaps Lee himself, attributed the failure at Bristoe to the mismanagement of, and lack of cooperation between, the Second and the Third Corps.[130] But whose job was it to coordinate the operations of the two commands? In fact, where was Robert E. Lee on the afternoon of October 14? According to Freeman, in the "mid-afternoon" Lee was riding with Ewell east of Greenwich near the lines of the Orange & Alexandria when they were "greeted with a heavy outburst of firing on the left, infantry and artillery—Hill evidently engaged hotly with the enemy."[131] Freeman then wrote: "Proceeding at once across country to ascertain the nature of the engagement, Lee did not arrive until the action was over."[132] Indeed, Hill's report makes no mention of the presence of the army commander; nor, for that matter, does Ewell's campaign diary entry for October 14.[133] But why did it take Lee so long to reach Hill, who was, at the most, two miles distant? The engagement began between 2:00 and 3:00 P.M. and lasted between three and four hours.[134] Lee should have been able to reach Hill within thirty minutes. Instead, at least three hours passed before the army commander reached Bristoe. Is it conceivable that Lee and his entire staff, mostly Virginians, could have lost their way and taken between three and four hours to cover two miles? Or was Lee physically overcome by the excitement of the moment? After all, he had been troubled earlier in the month by severe attacks of angina pectoris.[135] There is thus a good chance that Lee was too ill to oversee the movements of either of his senior lieutenants. Whatever the truth, the fact remains that Lee missed the entire battle of Bristoe Station, and in his absence both Ewell and Hill were left to their own devices and their own interpretations of whatever it was that Lee hoped to extract from the campaign. Did Lee's corps commanders understand, any better than historians writing in the twentieth century, just what Lee's objectives for the October 1863 effort were? What risks ought to be taken in an effort to bring on an engagement? If Lee's ultimate goal was to gain space or time, then it mattered little whether Hill engaged the Federals before they crossed Broad Run. But if battle *was* central to Lee's campaign strategy, as the memoirs of Jubal Early suggest, then the retreat across the run had to be interrupted before the Federal rear guard made good its escape. An obviously frustrated Taylor, in a letter written to his wife the day after the engagement at Bristoe, lamented the fact that "we will not be able to force them to a battle," implying that Lee's aim had been to do just that—to force a battle.[136]

Lee's offensive-mindedness caused his army yet another reverse on November 7 at Rappahannock Crossing. As Lee retraced his steps after Bristoe, he directed Ewell's Second Corps to fortify a "*tête-du-pont*" on the north bank of the river near the destroyed rail crossing at Rappahannock Station. In a report for President Davis written after the loss of the position, Lee wrote that he established the bridgehead for defensive reasons, "with the view of deterring [Meade], if possible, from advancing farther into the interior this winter."[137] The existence of a Confederate enclave on the north bank of the river would complicate any Federal offensive, but only if Meade attempted to cross the river and to contain or eliminate the bridgehead simultaneously. What if Meade undertook these two tasks in succession? Even a sympathetic biographer, Douglas Southall Freeman, believed that Lee was thinking offensively, rather than defensively, and viewed the *tête-du-pont* not as a means to break up a Federal offensive, but as a bridgehead from which the Army of Northern Virginia might launch a future assault.[138] Lee clung stubbornly to the hope that he would be able to resume the offensive. He wrote his wife on October 25: "General Meade, I believe, is repairing the railroad, and I presume will come on again. If only I could get some shoes and clothes for the men, I would save him the trouble."[139]

At Lee's direction, Ewell fortified the *tête-du-pont*, garrisoned alternately by the divisions of the Second Corps. At least one of the division commanders responsible for the security of the bridgehead, Major General Jubal A. Early, disliked the idea of holding a position on the north bank of the Rappahannock. He believed that the *tête-du-pont* could be made strong, but only with extensive engineering support that was not forthcoming from army headquarters.[140]

Early's concerns were justified. On November 7, in a rare night attack, the Federals struck, surprising both Lee and Early, capturing the bridgehead and the bulk of two brigades from the latter's division—the garrison force, Brigadier General Harry T. Hays's Louisiana brigade, and Brigadier General Robert F. Hoke's North Carolina brigade, which had reinforced the bridge-head earlier in the day.[141] Walter Taylor wrote of the debacle that very night in a letter to his wife, describing the day's events as "the saddest chapter in the history of this army."[142]

Lee had suffered another defeat, albeit a minor one, in the short and sharp action at Rappahannock Station. The Army of Northern Virginia lost 2,023 men, this time in Early's division of Ewell's Second Corps.[143] As at Bristoe, two brigades alone bore the entire effort. "We had no support or re-inforcements," one survivor later recalled.[144] "The wisdom of the generalship by which our two brigades were placed on the north bank of a deep river to meet the advance of a great army," he also noted, "is not apparent."[145]

As Lee marched back over the Rapidan, almost a month to the day from the beginning of his advance from Orange Court House, he had accomplished little. The offensive had deci-mated the Army of Northern Virginia—the four thousand casu-alties represented about 10 percent of its strength. More im-portant, four of Lee's twenty-seven infantry brigades (three from North Carolina) had been all but destroyed. Moreover, be-cause of the somewhat hasty withdrawal that followed the ac-tion at Bristoe Station, Lee's men were unable to gather up the substantial supplies abandoned by Meade's retreating army. As John Cheeves Haskell, then a major commanding one of the army's reserve artillery battalions, recalled: "[Bristoe] was a most unfortunate blunder, as it cost us a good many men and we lost large stores which would have been most valuable to us."[146]

In Richmond, Kean, the head of the Bureau of War, declared the Bristoe campaign "fruitless."[147] The mishap along the Rappahannock further diminished Lee's reputation in Kean's mind. He wrote on November 9: "On Friday General Lee suffered a severe loss in Hays's Louisiana and Hoke's North Carolina brigades, which were overpowered and captured at Rappahannock Bridge. This again must have been the result of bad management; General Lee's losses of late have greatly exceeded what he has inflicted."[148]

THE BRISTOE STATION CAMPAIGN demonstrates that despite the disaster at Gettysburg, Lee had remained wedded to the offensive. He could easily have remained on the defensive and allowed Meade to attack across the Rapidan. Reading Lee's correspondence of August and September 1863 with Davis and Seddon, one might assume that Lee had never before successfully held off a numerically superior army, and that the commander of the Army of Northern Virginia had forgotten his successes at Fredericksburg and Chancellorsville. As J. F. C. Fuller noted: "Whilst *Lee's* offensive distributions were frequently faulty, seldom well organized and generally badly staffed, his defensive distributions, especially when fighting Grant in 1864, were admirable."[149] In June 1863, Lee marched north with about seventy-seven thousand men against Meade's army, a force of ninety thousand men who had not fully recovered from the debacle at Chancellorsville. But for Lee to attack an army twice the size of his own in October was absurd. He marched north with nothing more than a hope that he might win some kind of meaningful, if only symbolic victory, but with a conviction that an offensive was the surest way to forestall further detachments from his own army. As Walter Taylor wrote on October 25: "As soon as it was evident that Meade would not fight us, there was much talk amongst officers and men of a probable detachment of another large slice of our old army for duty in Tennessee."[150] But, as Taylor suspected, the season was too advanced for such transfers. Lee, through his abortive offensive, had once again forced the strategic hands of his government.

Conclusions

"More Mighty Than He Seems"

Aꜰᴛᴇʀ ʟᴇᴇ's ꜰᴀɪʟᴇᴅ ʙʀɪꜱᴛᴏᴇ ꜱᴛᴀᴛɪᴏɴ ᴄᴀᴍᴘᴀɪɢɴ, he never again had the opportunity to undertake another strategic offensive. Nevertheless, his desire to crush the Federal troops arrayed against the Army of Northern Virginia remained central to his strategic outlook. Even in the spring of 1864, as powerful Federal armies tightened their vise-like grip on a weakened Confederacy, Lee still searched for the opportunity, as he termed it, "to strike an offensive blow." "We must destroy this army of Grant's before he gets to James River," Lee advised Major General Jubal A. Early, then commanding a corps along the North Anna River. "If he gets there, it will become a siege, and then it will be a mere question of time."[1]

While there exists a consensus among historians of the American Civil War regarding Lee's affinity for the offensive, there remain divisions with respect to the propriety of his strategic concept, given the situation confronting the South. Lee's critics portray him as the man who helped to ensure that the Confederacy lost the war. As Russell F. Weigley argued in his classic *The American Way of War,* Lee "destroyed in the end not the enemy armies, but his own."[2] Conversely, Lee's defenders suggest that the Virginia general almost achieved the impossible, only in the end to be, as Jubal Early concluded, "worn down by the combined agencies of numbers, steampower, railroads, mechanism, and all the resources of physical science."[3]

Weigley is but one of several eminent historians to challenge Lee's reputation. Many others have likewise questioned the wisdom of his relentlessly aggressive "Napoleonic" tactics in an era of rifled muskets and artillery.[4] Some have portrayed his focus on the war in the eastern theater less as a well thought-out strategic choice than as evidence of his Virginia parochialism. Still others have suggested that Lee paid too little attention to the important but less glamorous aspects of generalship, such as paperwork, staffing, organization, and logistics.

The many who, along with Early, view Lee as one of the great—if not *the* greatest—commanders of the age, consider his victories clear evidence of his tactical genius; his focus on the eastern theater the result of a keen understanding of geography and political realities north and south of the Potomac; and his quest for a decisive battle fought on Northern soil reflective of sound, traditional strategy and the peculiarities and fundamental weaknesses of Southern society. Lee's ultimate failure is attributed to a combination of overwhelming odds, misfortune on the field of battle, and to less than wholehearted support from his civilian superiors, most notably President Jefferson Davis, as well as his principal subordinates, most especially James Longstreet.

Who is right—Lee's critics or his defenders? Any effort to answer that question must begin with another: Could the South have won the Civil War? After all, if the answer to that question is negative, then the historical debate concerning Confederate strategy becomes moot.

The North possessed innumerable advantages over the South. The Federal government had at its disposal a larger population, greater and more diverse industrial production, a far more extensive network of railroads along with an industrial infrastructure to maintain them, both coastal and oceanic shipping, powerful naval forces, an existing bureaucratic governmental structure, and a diverse and productive agricultural sector. On paper, the South appears to have stood little chance in the war.

But the Confederacy possessed several advantages. Early in the war the ranks of its armies, at least those deployed in the East, were filled by soldiers better motivated and, especially, better led than their Northern adversaries. For the most part, Southern troops fought on familiar terrain in defense of their homes. Most important, the asymmetry of the war favored the rebellion, for the struggle was not a true civil war. The South did not intend—and did not need—to conquer the North to "win." The Confederacy had only to survive until the Yankees lost their will to continue the struggle.

To a great extent, this last-named advantage offset the many possessed by the Union. While the North controlled the greater pool of resources, President Abraham Lincoln faced a far more difficult challenge than did Jefferson Davis. Lincoln had not simply to defeat the South, but to conquer, occupy, and subdue an area roughly the size of western and central Europe combined. He had no more than four years to complete, or at least to make significant progress toward, this object before he faced reelection in the fall of 1864. We know that Lincoln assumed that he could conceivably face political defeat, and at one point in the late summer of 1864 actually thought that he would not be reelected.

History also provides support for the view that the South could, or perhaps even should, have won the contest. The material advantages of the North were significant, but so, too, were those possessed by the British over the Americans in 1775–1783, the Americans over the Vietnamese in Indochina in the mid-1960s, and the Soviets over the Afghans in Afghanistan in the 1980s. In the American War Between the States, a combination of Northern failure and Confederate success, if not probable, was at least possible.

If so, what strategy should the South have pursued? Here again history offers a guide, for the record of past wars demonstrates that there are two basic strategies that a nation at war can employ. The first seeks the decisive defeat of the enemy's armies in battle as a means to destroy his capability to resist; the second endeavors, through a variety of means, to exhaust the enemy's will and ability to continue the struggle.

The German military historian Hans Delbrück termed the former *Niederwerfungs-Strategie;* that is, the strategy of overthrow or annihilation. Historians generally associate this approach to the making of war with the work of the Prussian soldier and military philosopher Carl von Clausewitz, whose classic *On War* was published posthumously in 1833. "*War,*" Clausewitz argued, "*is . . . an act of force to compel our enemy to do our will.*"[5]

To Clausewitz, the natural state to which war tended was the absolute—a total and unrestrained effort to destroy one's enemy. He formulated a pair of interrelated principles, writing that the "destruction of the enemy's forces is generally accomplished by means of great battles and their results; and, the primary object of great battles must be the destruction of the enemy's forces."[6]

But before his death Clausewitz recognized that his focus on absolute war was too constricted and that any effort to produce a universal philosophy of war had to account for the myriad situations, so evident in the historical record, in which states waged limited, or less than total war. For Clausewitz the term "limited" could mean the pursuit of something other than the total overthrow of an enemy state, or a military effort constrained by inadequate resources that ruled out a more aggressive, unlimited strategy.[7]

Clausewitz died before he resolved this inconsistency in his work, and it fell to Hans Delbrück to more clearly define what he termed *Ermattungs-Strategie.* Many American writers, especially those in the military, translate Delbrück's term as "strategy of attrition," connoting, unfortunately, efforts to weaken an enemy's force through a lengthy process of trading casualties. But until the post–World War II era, most scholars—for example, Gordon Craig in his essay on Delbrück in *Makers of Modern*

Strategy (1943)—translated the term *Ermattungs-Strategie* as the "strategy of exhaustion."[8] In fact, proper translation of the German verb *ermatten* is not to abrade, but to tire, to exhaust, to weary, to weaken, or to wear down, all of which provide one with a better idea of what Delbrück had in mind than the term "attrition."

Delbrück recognized a variety of measures that a commander could adopt to weaken, either physically or morally, an enemy without having to seek as a primary goal the engagement and destruction of his main army. He did not rule out the possibility that at a subsequent stage of the war or campaign of exhaustion a climactic battle could be fought. Delbrück wrote:

> The possibility of forcing the enemy to such an extent, even without battle, that he accepts the conditions sought by our side leads in its ultimate degree to a pure maneuver strategy that allows war to be conducted without bloodshed. *Such a pure maneuver strategy, however, is only a dialectical game and not any real event in world military history.* . . . The possibility of a decision by battle therefore always remains in the background, even with those commanders who wish to avoid bloodshed, and so the strategy of attrition [exhaustion] is not at all to be equated with a pure strategy of maneuver; rather, it is to be regarded as a type of warfare that is hostage to an internal contradiction. Its principle is a polarized one or one with a double pole.[9]

Delbrück actually preferred the term "bipolar" or "two-poled strategy" to "strategy of exhaustion." For Delbrück, the two strategic poles were battle and maneuver. He did not envision his strategy of exhaustion as one that sought to avoid battle; it was simply a strategy adopted when a strategy of annihilation was impossible, perhaps because the enemy's main force was too strong, or the aim of destroying the opposing army was impractical, or unnecessary, for political reasons.

Which strategic approach ought the South to have pursued? If the American Civil War was a struggle for national liberation on the part of the Confederacy, the South should have pursued a strategy of exhaustion: a primarily defensive, though by no means passive, effort to wear down or exhaust Northern political resolve. In strategic terms, the South lacked not only the means, but also the necessity to embark upon a more aggressive *and* demanding strategy of annihilation. As Steven E. Woodworth has shown in his *Davis and Lee at War,* Confederate President Jefferson Davis favored a strategic approach that sought the exhaustion of the Northern will to continue the war.[10]

But were the rebellious Southerners waging a true war of national liberation? While the resiliency of the Lost Cause ideal suggests that they were, not all historians agree. The authors of *Why the South Lost the Civil War* argued that "the Confederacy succumbed to internal rather than external causes." They concluded that an "insufficient nationalism failed to survive the strains imposed by the lengthy hostilities."[11]

If, in fact, Southern wartime nationalism was not as strong as the postwar allure for the Confederacy suggests, Lee's quest for a quick and "decisive" end to the war reflected sound strategy. If the elements of matériél *and* time were both working against the Southern cause, as Gary Gallagher has argued, the situation justified the adoption of what might be termed a strategy of annihilation.[12] Under such circumstances the Confederacy had to strike a decisive blow before the North could fully mobilize its overwhelming resources and itself employ a strategy of exhaustion against the South.

Who, then, was right—Jefferson Davis or Robert E. Lee? After more than a century of research and writing, Civil War historians remain divided. And for good reason: no historian, no economist, no political scientist, no human being can say with metaphysical certainty that Davis *or* Lee was correct.

It is entirely conceivable that the South should have adopted Davis's strategy of exhaustion. After all, had Lee remained on the strategic defensive following Second Bull Run and Chancellorsville, additional resources and manpower could have been deployed to other theaters, possibly to advantage as the Confederates demonstrated in the fall of 1863 during the Chickamauga campaign. What if Longstreet's corps had gone west not on the heels of the debacle at Gettysburg and the fall of Chattanooga, but immediately after Lee's great victory at Chancellorsville? How might the outcome of the Federal election of 1864 have differed had the Union's string of successes in the western theater been broken, if only temporarily, and had Atlanta not fallen to Major General William Tecumseh Sherman's armies in September 1864?

Alternatively, we can speculate about the possible course of events had McClellan not found the Lost Dispatch and Lee had more time to reconcentrate his army along Antietam Creek before the Federals attacked in mid September 1862. How might the Gettysburg campaign have played out had Jackson lived, or had Jefferson Davis more fully supported Lee's plan to invade Pennsylvania and formed an additional corps under Beauregard near Culpeper? What would have been the political and international impact of the equivalent of a Second Manassas or Chancellorsville won on Northern soil in 1862 or 1863?

While history cannot tell us definitively whether the strategic predilections of Jefferson Davis or Robert E. Lee were best suited to the situation confronting the Confederacy, the documentary record does demonstrate one fact quite clearly: the Confederate government failed to adopt and to pursue steadfastly either a strategy of exhaustion or a strategy of annihilation. The Southern cause, without a doubt, would have been better served if either strategy—be it Davis's or Lee's—had been executed consistently.

Jefferson Davis is certainly culpable for this failure to adopt a coherent strategy. As commander in chief of the Confederate armed forces, Davis bore the responsibility both to shape, and to ensure that his field commanders faithfully adhered to, a well-defined national strategy. This Davis clearly failed to do.

But if Davis was the Confederacy's chief strategic culprit, what of the role of Robert E. Lee, the president's principal military adviser and commander of the South's most important army? Historians, unfortunately, have generally asked the wrong question—namely, "Was Lee right?" Gary Gallagher, for example, made a strong case in support of Lee's strategy in his essay "Another Look at the Generalship of Robert E. Lee," recently republished in the anthology *Lee: The Soldier.* But Gallagher missed the point: right or wrong Lee was just that—a soldier—and not the Confederate commander in chief.

When on campaign, it was Lee's job to implement, not to reshape, Confederate strategy. But as Lee's movements and correspondence in September 1862, following his victory at Second Manassas, between April and June 1863, before the start of the Gettysburg campaign, and again in October 1863 as his army marched toward Bristoe Station demonstrate, the commander of the Army of Northern Virginia was determined to force Davis's strategic hand. In so doing, Lee usurped Davis's role as commander in chief.

If Lee's behavior after Second Manassas was an isolated event, he could be forgiven by the historian, as he was by Davis. The impulse to retain the initiative after a successful campaign was understandably enormous. Any commander worth his pay would certainly have considered a Northern invasion in an effort to maintain the favorable tempo of operations. But, as the course of future events showed, Lee's behavior on the eve of the Maryland campaign was not an exception, but the rule. In the spring of 1863 Lee never fully disclosed his plans for his invasion of Pennsylvania to Davis or the cabinet. In October 1863, Lee lied about the location and the movements of the army to the secretary of war.

But assuming that Lee's was the correct strategy for the Confederacy, was he not thus doing his nation a service? The answer to that question is clear: He was not. Lee's determination to mold Confederate strategy into a form more to his liking led him to keep his true intentions hidden from President Davis and the cabinet. To keep the government in the dark, Lee had to prevent the details of his plans from reaching Richmond in the form of rumors. In an age that predated the concept of official secrets, Lee could only ensure that end by refusing to share his plans with his senior lieutenants and the members of his staff.

As a result, Lee launched all three of his strategic offensives without anything approaching a formal plan. Lee, of course, could not possibly have drawn up a detailed plan that accounted for the movements of each and every unit in the Army of Northern Virginia as they moved from the Rappahannock to the Susquehanna. As Clausewitz wrote: "It is rare, or at any rate uncommon, for a general to set out with a firm objective in mind; rather, he will make it dependent on the course of events."[13] No plan, as the General Helmuth von Moltke (The Elder) reminded us, "survives contact with the enemy."[14] Nevertheless, a commander intent on launching an offensive ought at least to possess a basic concept of operations: to decide whether his principal goal is geographic or military—to take or reach a place, or to meet, engage, and hopefully destroy an enemy army.

In Lee's eagerness to keep his plans secret from his political superiors, he also denied to himself the additional support that he required to enable his plans to work. An unwillingness in the spring of 1863 to forthrightly argue the case with Davis and the Confederate cabinet for the creation of a corps of observation under Beauregard in northern Virginia undermined Lee's own plans for invasion. Admittedly, Lee might well have undermined his own arguments against the utility of the transfer of troops from his army to the West had he argued for the transfer of troops from the coastal Carolinas. Had Davis and the cabinet more fully understood, as did Lee, the risks he believed ought to be run to support fully his invasion plan, perhaps they would have sent Longstreet west in early June 1863. For these reasons, Lee, while he suggested the creation of a new command in northern Virginia under Beauregard before and after the May 16 meeting with the cabinet, did not insist on it during that conference. Instead, Lee accepted what was for him a compromise position that ensured that he would win the debate, but did little to acquire the forces that he believed necessary to secure success. Similarly, in October 1863, Lee was unwilling to demand the resources that his planned offensive required, despite the fact that his army was woefully equipped and supplied, for fear that Davis or Seddon, rather than ordering the quartermaster to provide proper support of the offensive, might have instead directed Lee to remain on the defensive. Instead, Lee undertook the Bristoe Station campaign with minimal preparation. His army was ill-equipped for a rapid, fall march through an area deficient in resources. Supplies were tight and the quartermaster's corps was not up to par. With the primary Confederate offensive continuing in Tennessee, Lee ought not to have been surprised that his heretofore immobile army failed to receive priority for supplies to conduct a drive, the timing and scope of which were unknown to the quartermaster's corps.

Lee's failure to commit anything approaching a detailed plan to paper also led to more than the disappointment and frustration of future historians of the American Civil War. Proper staffing—the efforts of more than a single individual to work out the details of a plan, if only in a general sense, on paper—reveals inconsistencies and ambiguities, thereby preventing potential misunderstandings, misinterpretations, and assorted other unforeseen complications. As the British historian and military analyst J. F. C. Fuller noted: "Lee disliked the minutiae of command, the need to communicate in writing with both subordinates and superiors, and the need to insure, through aggressive actions, not occasional letter writing, that his army was paid, fed, shod, and clothed."[15] Or as Taylor, one of Lee's staff officers, wrote, the commander of the Army of Northern Virginia "had a great dislike to reviewing army communications."[16]

Had Lee drawn up and staffed a plan for his June 1863 march to the Potomac, Longstreet would not have prematurely led his corps into the valley. Perhaps an additional cavalry brigade would have preceded Ewell's corps into Maryland, avoiding the problem that arose when Lee directed Stuart on June 23 to take his horsemen from the rear to the van of the army. Had Lee made better use of his staff, perhaps Fitz Lee's division of cavalry, and not A. P. Hill's infantry, would have led the march to Bristoe.

Lee's unwillingness to share his plans with his subordinates (other than Jackson) also proved to be extremely counterproductive in an army that relied upon a rather decentralized approach to command and control. Lee's secretiveness thickened what military historians term "the fog of war." As Clausewitz wrote:

> . . . all action takes place, so to speak, in a kind of twilight, which like fog or moonlight, often tends to make things seem grotesque and larger than they really are.
>
> Whatever is hidden from full view in this feeble light has to be guessed at by talent, or simply left to chance. So once again for lack of objective knowledge one has to trust to talent or luck.[17]

Lee's lieutenants, with their commander's plans "hidden from full view," often found themselves with no recourse but to guess what it was they were supposed to do when unforeseen circumstances arose. Stonewall Jackson is reported to have said of Lee: "He is the only man whom I would follow blindfold."[18] Jackson's remark, even if apocryphal, is germane, for the Army of Northern Virginia's corps commanders often did have to follow Lee even though they were denied insight into his intentions. Unfortunately for Lee and the Confederacy, Ewell and Hill lacked the requisite "talent" to operate while effectively blindfolded; if Longstreet and Stuart possessed the means, they nevertheless had the bad "luck" to choose wrong.

During the Maryland campaign, the fact that Lee's commanders did not fully comprehend his intentions made little difference. Little more than a week after crossing the Potomac, the Army of Northern Virginia found itself at Sharpsburg with its back to the river. At that point, every officer from the commanders of the wings down to the individual regiments arrayed along Antietam Creek understood their mission. But during the course of the Gettysburg campaign, time and again Lee's four senior lieutenants found themselves less than certain about just what it was that they were expected to do. Longstreet, Ewell, and Stuart all made decisions that undermined Lee's efforts, decisions that they might not have made have they more fully appreciated Lee's plans. Only Hill avoided serious miscalculation, but in that he was saved only by Lee's frequent presence at his headquarters during the morning of July 1, 1863. When Hill was left on his own—for example, on October 14—he, too, miscalculated and the results were grave.

Of course, to argue that Lee should have shared his plans with his subordinates assumes that he possessed plans to share. Given the near-total absence of documentation regarding Lee's strategic offensives, it is entirely possible, if not likely, that he launched all three without anything approaching what could be termed a proper plan, even in his own mind. The possibility exists that Lee's planning went no further than a determination to move north and see what happened—a determination reinforced in the spring, summer, and fall of 1863 by a realization that if he did not march, Federal inactivity would lead to the detachment of troops from the Army of Northern Virginia for service on other fronts. Lee placed his trust in his own abilities, his God, and an expectation that his Federal opponent—be it McClellan, Hooker, or Meade—would somehow contribute to his own demise.

While some historians have criticized Lee's style of warfare for being too Napoleonic, with regard to strategy and planning they do the infamous Corsican a disservice. Napoléon never undertook a major strategic offensive without some kind of formal plan. When he set out to shatter the Third Coalition in 1805, he did not march his army across the Rhine and into Bavaria with nothing more than an intention to carry the war into enemy territory, victual his army in Germany, and then to wait and see how the Austrians and their Russian allies reacted. Napoléon's late summer march from the English Channel to the Rhine, and thence to the Danube, was well thought out, had a clearly identified objective (the destruction of the Austrian army at Ulm), had been thoroughly planned and staffed, and was understood, to some extent, by all of the emperor's senior lieutenants.[19]

Nothing in Lee's education and early experience as a soldier would have taught him to act otherwise. At the United States Military Academy at West Point, his reading of the works of Antoine-Henri Jomini could have convinced Lee that governments ought to allow their ablest military commander a free hand to wage war as he saw fit and of the primacy of the offensive, but Jomini was a proponent of several concepts that Lee preferred on occasion to forget: the strategic advantages of the use of interior lines and a scientific approach to the study of warfare and the execution of the campaign. Jomini's reputation, after all, rested on his work as a staff officer and not a field commander.[20] Nor would Lee's service during the Mexican War have suggested to him that an offensive campaign ought to be conducted without a clearly defined objective or a concept of operations. During the latter part of the war Lee served on the staff of Major General Winfield Scott at Veracruz and on the march to Mexico City. Long before the first surf boats headed toward the Mexican coast, Scott had drawn up an outline plan entitled "Vera Cruz and Its Castle—New Line of Operations, Thence Upon the Capital."[21] Lee found Scott a diligent commander who took great lengths to ensure the supply of his army, who was often, as Freeman noted, "deep in conferences with the commanders," and who was determined to reach Mexico City to force an end to the war.[22] When the then Captain Lee served as the guide for one of Scott's divisions at the battle of Cerro Gordo on April 17, 1848, he knew more of his commander's plans and intentions than would Longstreet, Ewell, and Hill—lieutenant generals all—on July 1, 1863![23]

Two lessons that Lee did apparently learn from his early experiences in command of the Army of Northern Virginia were that he possessed the ability to quickly adjust his own operations to changing circumstances and that the Federal commanders were unable to do the same. After bullying the much larger army of McClellan out of the Peninsula, and chasing Pope's back to the outskirts of Washington, Lee thereafter assumed the incompetence of his opponents. In the Maryland, Gettysburg, and Bristoe Station campaigns, Lee moved north without a firm plan of action, expecting—or hoping—that during the course of the operation the Federal commander would make a misstep and allow Lee an opportunity to seize the moment. But it was Lee who miscalculated in September 1862; Ewell and Stuart who blundered in June and July 1863; Hill who misjudged at Bristoe; and Early and Lee, both of whom were positioned on a hill overlooking the bridgehead, who incorrectly assumed that Meade would never launch a night assault at Rappahannock Station. In his memoirs, Early admitted as much, writing: "In constructing these works too great reliance had been placed in the want of enterprise on the part of the enemy."[24] The British military historian and analyst J. F. C. Fuller noted: "[Lee] undervalued the valour of his adversaries, though he read like a book the character of many of their generals, and on the whole had the highest contempt for their abilities."[25] Or, as William Shakespeare's Henry V cautioned:

> 'Tis best to weigh
> The enemy more mighty than he seems.[26]

LEE'S TWIN PENCHANTS for the offensive and for secrecy contorted the outlines of Confederate national strategy between 1862 and 1863 and led to his own failures as a commander. To be sure, Jefferson Davis approved of Lee's decision to invade Maryland in September 1862, but only after the fact, for the general had given the president no choice but to acquiesce. And Lee won an open strategic debate in the spring of 1863, but only by adopting a less-than-frank line of argument concerning the resources he needed to make his strategy work, and by overselling its likely impact on the course of the war in the western theater. When the Gettysburg campaign failed, and Vicksburg fell, Lee was forced to detach troops to the West. But he did not hunker down in a defensive posture. Without providing any forewarning to the authorities in Richmond, Lee embarked on yet another offensive—in part, at least, to forestall additional detachments from the army.

What Lee did not comprehend, and most historians have never understood, is that his desire to shape, as well as to implement, Confederate grand strategy from his headquarters in northern Virginia forced him to embrace a cloak of secrecy about his plans that, to be sure, enabled him to conduct his operations without undue interference from Richmond, but not without a price. When Robert E. Lee led the Army of Northern Virginia on its three strategic offensives of 1862 and 1863, the pressures of those operations not only amplified the weaknesses evident in the army, and in Lee's own character and style of generalship, but also produced an unappreciated synergistic effect. A general and an army that were magnificent when fighting on the defensive faltered when on the strategic offensive, because secrecy concerning the army's plans bred uncertainty, hesitation, and miscalculation—not just in Richmond, not just in the minds of Lee's subordinates, but also in his own mind. Even Lee did not know what he was about when he moved north. He was uncertain about which course to pursue when he learned that McClellan was at Frederick in September 1862. Lee was uncertain whether or not he wished to bring on a general engagement on the morning and afternoon of July 1, 1863. And Lee was unable to provide any direction to Hill as he blundered forward toward Bristoe Station on the afternoon of October 14, 1863.

Many of the characteristics evident in Lee's record as a commander—his ability to improvise, virtually without staff work, a plan of action in the midst of an ongoing operation; his faith that his subordinate commanders would react on their own initiative in response to developing circumstances; his relative lack of dependence on a cumbersome line of supply—worked to his advantage when his army stood on the strategic defensive and allowed an outnumbered but never outgeneraled Army of

Northern Virginia to embarrass and defeat the march larger Federal forces sent against it. But once Lee's army went over to the strategic offensive, these same traits abraded the effectiveness of the army. Lee and his lieutenants, campaigning without clearly defined objectives, often found themselves confused when circumstances developed along unforeseen lines, and for an army operating without anything approaching a well-staffed plan, every circumstance could be considered unforeseen. An army that reacted with celerity on the defensive, instead staggered and fell of its own weight on the offensive. The British soldier and historian G. F. R. Henderson wrote: "The Army of Northern Virginia became a different and less manageable instrument after Chancellorsville. Over and over again it failed to respond to the conceptions of its leader, and the failure was not due to the soldiers, but to the generals."[27] Indeed, Lee and his lieutenants did fail their men. But while the outcomes of the two campaigns—Gettysburg and Bristoe Station—that followed Lee's May 1863 victory along the south bank of the Rappahannock River support Henderson's observation, he nevertheless missed a critical point: Lee's army did, in fact, "respond" well in the defensive campaigns and battles of the spring and summer of 1864, whereas it had faltered before Chancellorsville, during the Maryland campaign of September 1862.

Robert E. Lee's strategic vision may well have been superior to that of President Jefferson Davis. Lee's strategy of invasion, and battle, may have offered the Confederacy its best hope of survival. But what Lee failed to understand was that a commander of an army can no more effectively shape national strategy on the sly, and on the cheap, than a tail can wag a dog.

Maps

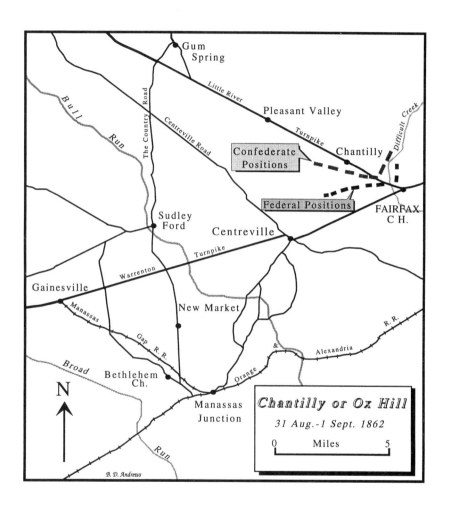

Gum
Spring

Bull
Run

The Country Road

Centreville Road

Little River

Pleasant Valley

Turnpike

Difficult Creek

Confederate
Positions

Chantilly

Federal Positions

FAIRFAX
C H.

Sudley
Ford

Centreville

Turnpike

Warrenton

Gainesville

Manassas

New Market

Gap R. R.

R. R.

Alexandria

Broad

&

Orange

Bethlehem
Ch.

N

Manassas
Junction

Run

B. D. Andrews

Chantilly or Ox Hill

31 Aug.-1 Sept. 1862

0   Miles   5

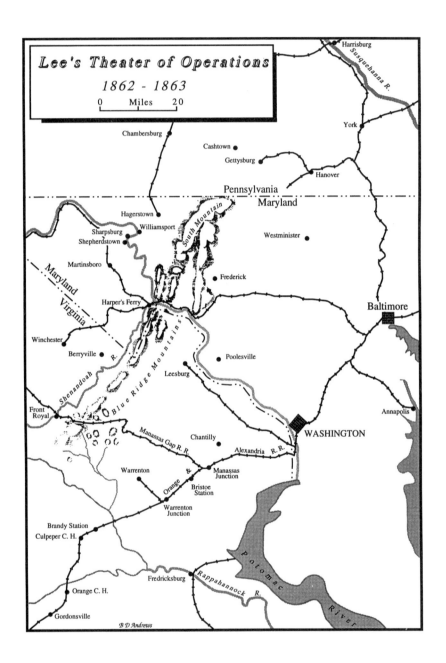

Lee's Theater of Operations
1862 - 1863

0   Miles   20

Harrisburg

Susquehanna R.

York

Chambersburg

Cashtown

Gettysburg

Hanover

Pennsylvania

Maryland

Hagerstown

Williamsport

Sharpsburg

Shepherdstown

South Mountain

Westminister

Martinsboro

Maryland

Virginia

Frederick

Harper's Ferry

Baltimore

Winchester

Berryville

Shenandoah R.

Blue Ridge Mountains

Poolesville

Leesburg

Annapolis

Front
Royal

Manassas Gap R. R.

Chantilly

Alexandria R. R.

WASHINGTON

Warrenton

Orange &

Manassas
Junction

Bristoe
Station

Warrenton
Junction

Brandy Station

Culpeper C. H.

Potomac

Fredricksburg

Rappahannock R.

River

Orange C. H.

Gordonsville

B D Andrews

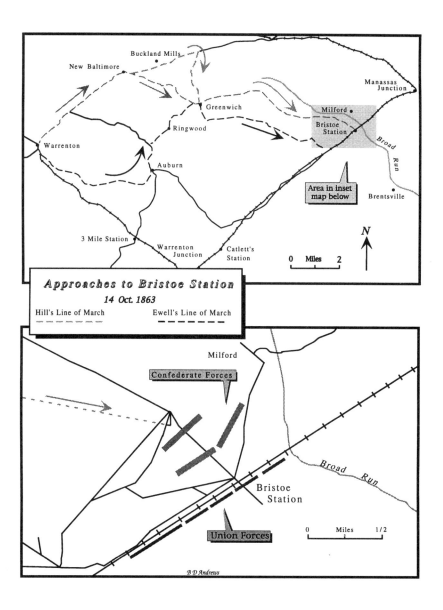

New Baltimore

Buckland Mills

Manassas
Junction

Greenwich

Milford

Warrenton

Ringwood

Bristoe
Station

Broad
Run

Auburn

Area in inset
map below

Brentsville

3 Mile Station

Warrenton
Junction

Catlett's
Station

N

0   Miles   2

Approaches to Bristoe Station
14 Oct. 1863

Hill's Line of March   Ewell's Line of March

Milford

Confederate Forces

Broad   Run

Bristoe
Station

Union Forces

0   Miles   1/2

B D Andrews

141

Notes

── **Preface** ──

1. John D. McKenzie, *Uncertain Glory: Lee's Generalship Re-Examined* (New York: Hippocrene, 1997), 350, argued that Lee "was a defensive military genius, but he preferred to use offensive strategies and tactics, areas in which he did not exhibit much expertise." The problem with this framework of interpretation is that Lee won his greatest victory—Chancellorsville—while conducting a tactical offensive. Lee also won at Second Manassas, where he engaged in offensive operations as well as a tactical offensive on the battlefield itself. Lee's problems began when he adopted a strategic offensive posture.

2. While General Robert E. Lee is one of the most venerated and respected figures of the American Civil War, he has not escaped criticism. From the postwar debates that began following the publication of veterans' memoirs, to the attack by Alan T. Nolan, the commander of the Army of Northern Virginia has come under periodic assault. For a sampling of historical writing critical of Lee see: the memoirs of one of Lee's most senior lieutenants, James Longstreet, *From Manassas to Appomattox: Memoirs of the Civil War in America* (1896; reprint, New York: Mallard Press, 1991); one of the first scholarly assaults, that of the British general and historian J. F. C. Fuller in his *Grant and Lee: A Study in Personality and Generalship* (New York: Scribner's, 1933); one of the most vituperative attacks on Lee's military capabilities, by the American historian Thomas L. Connelly in his "Robert E. Lee and the Western Confederacy: A Criticism of Lee's Strategic Ability," *Civil War History* 15 (June 1969): 116–132; Albert Castel's rejoinder, "The Historian and the General: Thomas L. Connelly versus Robert E. Lee," *Civil War History* 16 (March 1970): 50–63; the sixth chapter in Russell F. Weigley's *The American Way of War: A History of United States Military Strategy and Policy* (New York: Macmillan, 1973), in which Weigley portrayed Lee as a general still trying to fight and win a Napoleonic tactical battle in a modern war; the

restated attacks on Lee's strategic ability in Connelly's broader study of Confederate strategy, coauthored with Archer Jones, *The Politics of Command: Factions and Ideas in Confederate Strategy* (Baton Rouge: Louisiana State University Press, 1973); Connelly's attacks on Lee as a general and a man in *The Marble Man: Robert E. Lee and His Image in American Society* (New York: Knopf, 1977), and, with Barbara L. Bellows, *God and General Longstreet: The Lost Cause and the Southern Mind* (Baton Rouge: Louisiana State University Press, 1982); Alan T. Nolan's highly critical *Lee Considered: General Robert E. Lee and Civil War History* (Chapel Hill: The University of North Carolina Press, 1991); and, most recently, McKenzie, *Uncertain Glory*. Emory M. Thomas, in the most recent profile of the commander of the Army of Northern Virginia, *Robert E. Lee: A Biography* (New York: W. W. Norton, 1995), offers a balanced, though critical, assessment of the man.

—— 1. The Maryland Campaign ——

1. R. Lockwood Tower, ed., *Lee's Adjutant: The Wartime Letters of Colonel Walter Herron Taylor, 1862–1865* (Columbia: University of South Carolina Press, 1995), 41. For an excellent recent account, see John H. Hennessy, *Return to Bull Run: The Campaign and Battle of Second Manassas* (New York: Simon & Schuster, 1993).

2. Both Jackson and Longstreet controlled multidivision commands that were de facto corps. Technically, the Confederate government did not establish a formal corps structure until after the battle of Sharpsburg. I have thus termed the two major commands "wings."

3. Private Memorandum, October 20, 1863, Richard Stoddert Ewell letterbook, 10–12, Perkins Library, Special Collections, Duke University, Durham, N.C.

4. U.S. War Department, *The War of the Rebellion: A Compilation of the Official Records of the Union and Confederate Armies*, 128 vols. in four series (Washington, D.C.: Government Printing Office, 1880–1901), series 1, vol. 12, pt. 2:497; hereafter cited as *OR*, with all citations referring to series 1.

5. Hennessy, *Return to Bull Run*, 411, wrote that Lee's objective was the "outright destruction of the Union army."

6. Ibid., 557, 743–744.

7. Douglas Southall Freeman, *R. E. Lee: A Biography*, 4 vols. (New York: Scribner's, 1935), 2:338.

8. There are innumerable biographies of Lee. The standard is Freeman's, and the most recent is by Emory M. Thomas.

9. Arthur James Lyon Fremantle, *The Fremantle Diary: Being the Journal of Lieutenant Colonel Arthur James Lyon Fremantle, Coldstream Guards, on His Three Months in the Southern States,* ed. Walter Lord (Boston: Little, Brown, 1954), 197.

10. For a standard account of the generalship of Jackson, see G. F. R. Henderson, *Stonewall Jackson and the American Civil War* (New York: Da Capo, 1988); for the most recent biography, see James I. Robertson Jr., *Stonewall Jackson: The Man, the Soldier, the Legend* (New York: Macmillan, 1997).

11. On a modern map, Jackson's route followed the McGraws Ridge Road, Virginia state road 659.

12. For Longstreet, see his memoirs, *From Manassas to Appomattox: Memoirs of the Civil War in America* (1896; reprint, New York: Mallard Press, 1991), 191; and Jeffry D. Wert, *General James Longstreet: The Confederacy's Most Controversial Soldier—A Biography* (New York: Simon & Schuster, 1993).

13. Wert, *Longstreet,* 168–173; Hennessy, *Return to Bull Run,* 362–366, 459–461.

14. Longstreet, *From Manassas to Appomattox,* 191.

15. For evidence of squabbling between Confederate units over the spoils of the battlefield, see Douglas Southall Freeman, *Lee's Lieutenants: A Study in Command,* 3 vols. (New York: Scribner's, 1943), 2:146–147.

16. R. L. Dabney, a major, served at the time as assistant adjutant general on Jackson's staff. In Dabney's biography of Stonewall, *Life and Campaigns of Lieut.-Gen. Thomas J. Jackson* (New York: Blecock, 1866), 542–544, he described the march to the Little River Turnpike as little more than the preliminary movement of the army toward the Potomac. See also G. Moxley Sorrel, *Recollections of a Confederate Staff Officer* (New York: W. S. Konecky, 1994), 103–104.

17. Sorrel, *Recollections of a Confederate Staff Officer,* 103–104.

18. Walter H. Taylor, *General Lee: His Campaigns in Virginia, 1861–1865* (Lincoln: University of Nebraska Press, 1994), 115.

19. Ibid.

20. Ibid.

21. Longstreet, *From Manassas to Appomattox,* 193.

22. Ibid.

23. James I. Robertson Jr., *General A. P. Hill: The Story of a Confederate Warrior* (New York: Random House, 1992), 127.

24. *OR,* 12/2:744.

25. Ibid., 12/3:770.

26. Henderson, *Stonewall Jackson,* 480.

27. *OR,* 12/3:771.

28. Ibid., 12/2:81, 82.

29. Porter must have sighted Longstreet's column, since he reported that it was headed north toward, he assumed, Leesburg. In fact, after sighting the Confederate column, Porter suggested to McClellan that the army should "protect the fords into Maryland." Ibid., 788.

30. Ibid., 84.

31. Ibid.

32. Ibid., 45, 84, 85.

33. According to most accounts, the day was overcast. But Heros von Borcke, in *Memoirs of the Confederate War for Independence,* 2 vols. (New York: Peter Smith, 1938), 1:170, states that the weather was "beautiful" in the morning and changed late in the day. The day must have been sunny enough to have dried out the roads, for the Federals could see the dust thrown up by Lee's marching columns. *OR,* 12/2:788.

34. Von Borcke, *Memoirs,* 1:170.

35. *OR,* 12/2:744.

36. Stephen W. Sears, ed., *The Civil War Papers of George B. McClellan: Selected Correspondence, 1860–1865* (New York: Ticknor & Fields, 1989), 425–426.

37. *OR,* 12/2:744.

38. *OR,* 12/2:744; Von Borcke, *Memoirs,* 1:170.

39. Von Borcke, *Memoirs,* 1:170.

40. William Augustus McClendan, *Recollections of War Times by an Old Veteran While under Stonewall Jackson and Lieutenant General James Longstreet, How I Got In, and How I Got Out* (Montgomery, Ala.: Paragon Press, 1909), 123.

41. According to the report of Brigadier General James H. Lane, who was commanding Branch's Brigade of Powell Hill's division, the fight at Ox Hill began at 4:00 P.M. According to Lee's report, it started later, at 5:00 P.M.

42. Freeman, *Lee's Lieutenants,* 2:131.

43. *OR,* 12/2:344, 414, 418–419.

44. Longstreet, *From Manassas to Appomattox,* 200, termed the Federal stand at Ox Hill "severe."

45. Ibid., 194.

46. For a contemporary view see Charles Marshall, *An Aide-de-Camp of Lee: Being the Papers of Colonel Charles Marshall, Sometime Aide-de-Camp, Military Secretary, and Assistant Adjutant-General on the Staff of Robert E. Lee, 1862–1865,* ed. Sir Frederick Maurice (Boston: Little, Brown, 1927), 141. For a more recent example, Emory Thomas, in his biography of Lee, wrote:

> Next morning [August 31, 1862] Lee was still seeking ways to exploit his victory; but several circumstances seemed to conspire against accomplishing the annihilation he sought. Once relieved

of his fantasies about what was happening, Pope led a competent withdrawal, and as his troops fell back, they fell in with reinforcements arriving from McClellan's army. Lee's soldiers, Jackson's men especially, were almost without rations and for the moment pretty well fought out. On September 1, for example, Jackson's wing spent most of the day marching only three miles, encountered a Federal force smaller in numbers at Chantilly, attacked the inferior enemy, and suffered a general repulse. Nor did the weather cooperate with Lee's zeal to press his advantage. Rain pelted the armies during the night (August 30–31) and continued the following day. Not only did sodden roads impede the pursuit; they made it more difficult for supplies to overtake the hungry Confederates. Much later Lee explained his inability to take better advantage of the situation quite simply, "My men had nothing to eat . . . they had nothing to eat for three days."

See Emory M. Thomas, *Robert E. Lee: A Biography* (New York: W. W. Norton, 1995), 255.

47. See the report of Brigadier General Jubal Early, commanding Ewell's division, in *OR*, 12/2:714–715.

48. See Jedediah Hotchkiss, *Make Me a Map of the Valley: The Civil War Journal of Stonewall Jackson's Topographer*, ed. Archie P. McDonald (Dallas: Southern Methodist University Press, 1973), 77.

49. McClendan, *Recollections of War Times*, 123.

50. *OR*, 12/2:714.

51. For a discussion of Jackson's failings during the Seven Days' see Freeman, *Lee*, 2:247–249. Some historians have also criticized Jackson for his unexplained battlefield paralysis at Second Manassas, where he delayed before supporting Longstreet's advance. See Hennessy, *Return to Bull Run*, 382.

52. Von Borcke, *Memoirs*, 1:169.

53. Ibid.

54. *OR*, 12/2:745, 749.

55. Nolan would also round up bullocks for Lee in the Shenandoah Valley in May 1863, weeks before the start of the Gettysburg campaign. *OR*, 25/2:819.

56. *OR*, 19/2:588.

57. Longstreet, *From Manassas to Appomattox*, 195.

58. See Robertson, *Stonewall Jackson*, 371, 581–582; and James A. Kegel, *North with Lee and Jackson: The Lost Story of Gettysburg* (Mechanicsville, Pa.: Stackpole, 1996), 40–43.

59. William Allan, "Memoranda of Conversations with Robert E. Lee," in *Lee: The Soldier*, ed. Gary W. Gallagher (Lincoln: University of Nebraska

Press, 1996), 7. See also Dabney, *Jackson*, 544–545. Dabney's discussion of this debate suggests that he was well aware of what was passing between Jackson and Lee.

60. Longstreet, *From Manassas to Appomattox*, 199–200.

61. A. L. Long, *Memoirs of Robert E. Lee: His Military and Personal History* (Edison, N.J.: Blue & Grey Press, 1983), 204.

62. The suggestion that Davis move Bragg's army to Virginia demonstrates that Lee had more in mind than just conducting a raid into Northern territory.

63. Clifford Dowdey and Louis H. Manarin, eds., *The Wartime Papers of R. E. Lee* (Boston: Little, Brown, 1961), 292–294.

64. *OR*, 19/2:591–592.

65. Lee's suggestion in his previous letter that Bragg's army might be transferred to Virginia strongly suggests that the commander of the Army of Northern Virginia envisioned his move as a major effort—an invasion—and not a mere "raid."

66. Longstreet, *From Manassas to Appomattox*, 336–337. Thomas, *Lee*, 20, termed Lee an "enigma," who "seldom if ever revealed himself while he lived. To understand him, it is necessary to look behind his words."

67. *OR*, 19/2:593–594.

68. Ibid., 593, 601, 606.

69. Quoted in Freeman, *Lee's Lieutenants*, 2:144. See also T. C. DeLeon, *Four Years in Rebel Capitals: An Inside View of Life in the Southern Confederacy, From Birth to Death* (Mobile, Ala.: Gossip Printing, 1890), 241.

70. The effect of the string of victories, most notably but not solely those of Lee and his army, is evident in J. B. Jones, *A Rebel War Clerk's Diary: At the Confederate States Capital*, ed. Howard Swiggett, 2 vols. (New York: Old Hickory Bookshop, 1935), 1:147–152.

71. Letter, September 9, 1862, George E. Waller Papers, Southern Historical Collection, Davis Library, University of North Carolina, Chapel Hill.

72. Freeman, *R. E. Lee*, 2:353 n.

73. Longstreet, *From Manassas to Appomattox*, 201.

74. Robert Underwood Johnson and Clarence Clough Buel, eds., *Battles and Leaders of the Civil War*, 4 vols. (Secaucus, N.J.: Castle, n.d.), 2:604–606.

75. Dabney, *Jackson*, 543.

76. See Allan, "Memoranda," 7–24; and Edward Clifford Gordon, "Memorandum of a Conversation with General R. E. Lee," in Gallagher, *Lee*, 25–27.

77. Allan, "Memoranda," 7.

78. Ibid., 8. Emphasis in the original.

79. Gordon, "Memorandum," 27 n.

80. *OR*, 19/1:814.

81. For Smith's dispatch on the battle, see *OR*, 16/1:931.

82. *OR*, 19/2:596.

83. Tower, *Taylor Letters*, 42–43.

84. *OR*, 19/2:600. Lee's suggestions also indicate that he considered his march across the Potomac as more than a raid.

85. "Civil War Incidents as Told by an Old Veteran from Memory," typescript, 1908, 5, A. J. Dula Papers, Perkins Library, Special Collections, Duke University, Durham, N.C.

86. H. C. Wall, box 16, Confederate States of America Archives, Army Units, North Carolina Regiments, Perkins Library, Special Collections, Duke University, Durham, N.C.

87. *OR*, 19/2:596.

88. Ibid.

89. Ibid. Just how bad is evident in a letter Lee sent to Jackson and Longstreet on September 22. Lee wrote:

> The depredations committed by this army, its daily diminution by straggling, and the loss of arms thrown aside as too burdensome by stragglers, makes it necessary for preservation itself, aside from considerations of disgrace and injury to our cause arising from such outrages committed upon our citizens, that greater efforts be made by our officers to correct this growing evil. It is feared that roll-calls are neglected, and officers of companies and regiments are ignorant of the true condition of their commands, and are unable to account properly for absentees.

90. Memoirs, vol. 10, 197–198, Berry Greenwood Papers, Southern Historical Collection, Davis Library, University of North Carolina, Chapel Hill.

91. *OR*, 19/2:602.

92. Dabney, *Jackson*, 549.

93. Ibid.

94. Longstreet, *From Manassas to Appomattox*, 202.

95. Sears, *McClellan Papers*, 428; Warren W. Hassler Jr., *General George B. McClellan: Shield of the Union* (Baton Rouge: Louisiana State University Press, 1957), 224.

96. Sears, *McClellan Papers*, 430.

97. Ibid., 438–439.

98. Ibid., 431–432.

99. Ibid., 441–442.

100. Ibid., 449–450.

101. Freeman, *Lee*, 2:410.

102. Hassler, *McClellan*, 243.

103. *OR*, 19/2:281.

104. In a pessimistic September 13 letter to Davis, Lee admitted that he had lost at least a third, and possibly as much as half, of his army to straggling and desertion. *OR*, 19/2:605–606, 606–607.

105. *OR*, 19/1:142.

106. Thomas, *Lee*, 259.

107. Ibid.

108. Dabney, *Jackson*, 570.

109. Freeman, *Lee*, 2:380.

110. Sears, *McClellan Papers*, 467.

111. Ibid., 470.

112. Tower, *Taylor Letters*, 44–45.

113. Ibid., 46.

114. Martin van Creveld, *Command in War* (Cambridge, Mass.: Harvard University Press, 1985), 6.

115. Longstreet, *From Manassas to Appomattox*, 220.

116. Tower, *Taylor Letters*, 44–45.

117. *OR*, 19/1:143.

118. Tower, *Taylor Letters*, 45–46.

___ 2. The Gettysburg Campaign ___

1. Clifford Dowdey and Louis H. Manarin, eds., *The Wartime Papers of R. E. Lee* (Boston: Little, Brown, 1961), 343–344.

2. Ibid.

3. R. L. Dabney, *Life and Campaigns of Lieut.-Gen. Thomas J. Jackson* (New York: Blecock, 1866), 595.

4. Dowdey and Manarin, *The Wartime Papers of R. E. Lee*, Lee Dispatches, 363–364.

5. Ibid., 364–365.

6. Ibid., 379–380.

7. Ibid., 388–390.

8. Jedediah Hotchkiss, *Make Me a Map of the Valley: The Civil War Journal of Stonewall Jackson's Topographer*, ed. Archie P. McDonald (Dallas: Southern Methodist University Press, 1973), 116.

9. Rembert Patrick, *Jefferson Davis and His Cabinet* (Baton Rouge: Louisiana State University Press, 1944), 132–154.

10. *OR*, 25/2:698–699.

11. Ibid., 708–709.

12. Ibid., 713–714.

13. Ibid., 720.

14. Ibid., 724–725. On April 27, Lee assured Davis that "the river [the Mississippi] cannot be used as a highway of commerce, so that they [the Federals] can derive no material benefit from it." Ibid., 752.

15. Ibid., 730, 735–736, 737–738, 740–741, 744–745, 752–753.

16. Jackson survived the amputation but succumbed to pneumonia on May 10.

17. William F. Fox, *Regimental Losses In The American Civil War, 1861–1865: A Treatise On The Extent And Nature Of The Mortuary Losses In The Union Regiments, With Full And Exhaustive Statistics Compiled From The Official Records On File In The State Military Bureaus And At Washington* (Albany, N.Y.: Albany Publishing, 1889), 540, 550.

18. *OR*, 25/2:782–783.

19. Ibid., 790.

20. Ibid.

21. Ibid.

22. Ibid., 791–792.

23. It is unclear whether Lee went to Richmond on his own, or was summoned to the capital by Davis.

24. For a discussion of the military and political pressures building on Davis at the time, see William C. Davis, *Jefferson Davis: The Man and His Hour* (New York: HarperCollins, 1991), 487–505; and Jefferson Davis, *The Rise and Fall of the Confederate Government*, 2 vols. (Richmond, Va.: Garrett and Massie, n.d.), 2:340–344.

25. J. B. Jones, *A Rebel War Clerk's Diary: At the Confederate States Capital*, ed. Howard Swiggett, 2 vols. (New York: Old Hickory Bookshop, 1935), 1:324.

26. John H. Reagan, *Memoirs: With Special Reference to Secession and the Civil War*, ed. Walter Flavius McCales (New York and Washington, D.C.: Neale Publishing, 1906), 120–122, 150–153. There is some dispute about the dates of the meetings Reagan discusses in his memoir. James A. Kegel, *North with Lee and Jackson: The Lost Story of Gettysburg* (Mechanicsville, Pa.: Stockpole, 1996), 201–202, argued that the meetings took place in Richmond on February 28. Reagan's biographer, Ben H. Procter, *Not without Honor: The Life of John H. Reagan* (Austin: University of Texas Press, 1962), 147–151; and Steven E. Woodworth, *Davis and Lee at War* (Lawrence: University of Kansas Press, 1995), 230–232, dated the meetings to the weekend of May 14–16. In my opinion, the context within which Reagan mentioned the meetings suggests the later date.

27. Reagan, *Memoirs*, 121.

28. Douglas Southall Freeman, *R. E. Lee: A Biography*, 4 vols. (New York: Scribner's, 1935), 3:15.

29. Ibid., 3:16.

30. Jones, *A Rebel War Clerk's Diary*, 1:328.

31. Ibid., 1:333.

32. For Hill's perspective on the question of detachments, see Hal Bridges, *Lee's Maverick General: Daniel Harvey Hill* (Lincoln: University of Nebraska Press, 1991), 162–194. At the time, Hill did not know of Lee's plan for an invasion of Pennsylvania. When Hill did learn of the plan in late June 1863, he considered the invasion "most unfortunate," and "folly." In a June 25 letter to his wife, Hill wrote: "Genl Lee is venturing on a very hazardous movement; and one that must be fruitless, if not disastrous." Hill, who believed that the situation at Vicksburg was much worse than the commanders were admitting, supported Seddon's strategy of detaching troops from Lee's army and sending them west to relieve that embattled city. See ibid., 189–190.

33. *OR*, 25/2:832–833.

34. Ibid., 841–843.

35. Edwin B. Coddington, *The Gettysburg Campaign: A Study in Command* (New York: Scribner's, 1968), 7.

36. *OR*, 25/2:841–843.

37. Ibid., 848–849.

38. Ibid., 27/2:293–294.

39. Ibid., 27/3:868–869.

40. Ibid., 874.

41. Robert Garlick Hill Kean, *Inside the Confederate Government: The Diary of Robert Garlick Hill Kean*, ed. Edward Younger (New York: Oxford University Press, 1957), 69; Jones, *A Rebel War Clerk's Diary*, 1:342.

42. *OR*, 27/2:295.

43. Ibid., 27/3:924–925.

44. Allan, "Memoranda of Conversations with Robert E. Lee," in *Lee: the Soldier*, ed. Gary W. Gallagher (Lincoln: University of Nebraska Press, 1996), 14.

45. *OR*, 27/3:930–931.

46. Ibid., 27/2:305–311.

47. Ibid., 313–325.

48. In fact, Lee made just that argument in a letter written in 1868. See J. William Jones, *Personal Reminiscences of General Robert E. Lee* (Baton Rouge: Louisiana State University Press, 1994), 266–267. So, too, did Jefferson Davis, *Rise and Fall*, 2:367, whose memoirs make no mention of any link

between Lee's Northern invasion and the situation in the western theater, and who concluded: "Thus closed the campaign in Pennsylvania. The wisdom of the strategy was justified by the result." Ibid., 377. For an example of the willingness of historians to accept Lee's argument at face value, see Thomas L. Connelly and Archer Jones, *The Politics of Command: Factions and Ideas in Confederate Strategy* (Baton Rouge: Louisiana State University Press), 128–129.

49. Freeman, *Lee*, 2:504.

50. Ibid., 3:18–19.

51. Allan, "Memoranda," 14.

52. Richard E. Beringer, Herman Hattaway, Archer Jones, and William N. Still Jr., *Why the South Lost the Civil War* (Athens: University of Georgia Press, 1986), 260. The chief proponent of the thesis that Lee's invasions were, in fact, nothing more than raids meant to upset Union plans is Archer Jones, whose most recent argument for that thesis can be found in his *Civil War Command and Strategy: The Process of Victory and Defeat* (New York: Free Press, 1992), 166–167.

53. Emory M. Thomas, *Robert E. Lee: A Biography* (New York: W. W. Norton, 1995), 288.

54. A. L. Long, *Memoirs of Robert E. Lee: His Military and Personal History* (Edison, N.J.: Blue & Gray Press, 1983), 269.

55. Charles Marshall, *An Aide-de-Camp of Lee: Being the Papers of Colonel Charles Marshall, Sometime Aide-de-Camp, Military Secretary, and Assistant Adjutant-General on the Staff of Robert E. Lee, 1862–1865*, ed. Sir Frederick Maurice (Boston: Little, Brown, 1927), 215.

56. Ibid., 185.

57. Ibid., 185–186.

58. Ibid., 186.

59. Kegel, *North with Lee and Jackson*, 281–292.

60. Elizabeth Longford, *Wellington: The Years of the Sword* (New York: Harper & Row, 1969), 279.

61. Horatio Nelson, *The Dispatches and Letters of Vice Admiral Lord Nelson*, ed. Nicholas Harris Nicolas, 7 vols. (London: H. Colburn, 1845), 4:90–91.

62. Martin van Creveld, *Command in War* (Cambridge, Mass.: Harvard University Press, 1985), 274.

63. Quoted in Longford, *Wellington*, 282.

64. See Freeman, *Lee*, 1:552–553.

65. While the difference between a defensive and an offensive posture may not at first glance seem significant, it is of extreme importance. Imagine yourself in command of a company of infantry at a bivouac. Along comes the regimental commander on his horse, and he directs you to follow with

your troops. He leads you to a bridge crossing a river and orders you to remain there. An hour later a column of enemy infantry appears on the road leading to the bridge. What do you do? Well, most commanders would assume, correctly, that their job was to hold the bridge. You do just that and an hour later the regimental commander reappears and congratulates you. But he also directs you to place your men into column, cross the bridge, and to march north in the direction of Burgsville, a small town located about five miles up the road. When your men reach a point halfway to the town, you reach some enemy entrenchments on either side of the road. Simultaneously, you see a column of enemy infantry maneuvering around your left flank. What course do you follow? Now that you are on the offensive, the possible courses of action are many. Do you try to force your way up the road through the entrenchments? Do you take your men off the road and march around the flank of the enemy position? Do you move to your left to engage the enemy troops on your own flank? Or do you retreat back to the bridge to prevent the enemy from getting between you and the river?

66. Abram David Pollock to his father, June 30, 1863, Abram David Pollock Papers, Southern Historical Collection, Davis Library, University of North Carolina, Chapel Hill.

67. For example, see Clifford Dowdey, *Lee* (New York: Bonanza Books, 1965), 361–362.

68. Henry Heth, *The Memoirs of Henry Heth*, ed. James L. Morrison Jr. (Westport, Conn.: Greenwood Press, 1974), 174.

69. *OR*, 27/2:305–311.

70. Ibid., 313–325.

71. Long, *Memoirs*, 275.

72. Allan, "Memoranda," 14. Emphasis in the original.

73. Douglas Southall Freeman, *Lee's Lieutenants: A Study in Command*, 3 vols. (New York: Scribner's, 1935), 3:6–18; 51–58.

74. *OR*, 27/3:692.

75. Ibid., 923.

76. The dispatch appears to contain an error, as if it should read, ". . . should he appear to be moving northward," and not ". . . should he appear not to be moving northward." If so, the same error appears in the version reprinted in Marshall, *Aide-de-Camp*, 208.

77. *OR*, 27/2:687–710.

78. W. W. Blackford, *War Years with Jeb Stuart* (New York: Scribner's, 1945), 222.

79. Jenkins's brigade of cavalry from the Shenandoah Valley crossed the Potomac with the Second Corps, but operated on Ewell's left. Stuart, in his report on the Gettysburg campaign, criticized Lee's failure to make use

of Jenkins's horsemen. Given the fact that any substantive threat to the Army of Northern Virginia would most likely come from the southeast, a case could be made that Lee should have posted Jenkins on Ewell's right, and not his left. Certainly, once Lee suspected that Stuart was riding around the Federals, the army commander could have redirected Jenkins's movement toward the east. Neither Ewell, who was never informed of Stuart's plan, nor Lee made the optimum use of Jenkins's cavalry.

80. Freeman, *Lee's Lieutenants*, 3:18.

81. *OR*, 27/3:905.

82. Ibid., 913.

83. For an itinerary of the movements of the Army of the Potomac, see ibid., 27/1:1140–1150.

84. Napoleon I, *The Military Maxims of Napoleon*, trans. George C. D'Aguilar (New York: Da Capo, 1995), 58.

85. Richard Stoddert Ewell, *The Making of a Soldier: Letters of General R. S. Ewell*, ed. Percy Gatling Hamlin (Richmond, Va.: Whittet & Shepperson, 1935), 118–120.

86. Quoted in Percy Gatling Hamlin, *"Old Bald Head" (General R. S. Ewell): The Portrait of a Soldier* (Strasburg, Va.: Shenandoah Publishing House, 1940), 137.

87. Ibid.

88. John B. Gordon, *Reminiscences of the Civil War* (Baton Rouge: Louisiana State University Press, 1993), 38.

89. Ibid.

90. Allan, "Memoranda," 11.

91. Gordon, *Reminiscences*, 38.

92. Ibid., 11.

93. Freeman, *Lee's Lieutenants*, 3:20–38.

94. See Allan, "Memoranda," 11; and Lee's letter to Davis of June 15, *OR*, 27/2:295. Other than Allan's memoranda, no documentation exists that would indicate that Lee was dissatisfied with Ewell's handling of the campaign in the valley. Freeman, *Lee's Lieutenants*, 3:37–38, argues that Ewell performed well in his drive down the valley.

95. For example see Thomas L. Connelly and Barbara L. Bellows, *God and General Longstreet: The Lost Cause and the Southern Mind* (Baton Rouge: Louisiana State University Press, 1982); and Glenn Tucker, *Lee and Longstreet at Gettysburg* (Indianapolis: Bobbs-Merrill, 1968).

96. James Longstreet, *From Manassas to Appomattox: Memoirs of the Civil War in America* (1896; reprint, New York: Mallard Press, 1991), 327–328.

97. Jeffry D. Wert, *General James Longstreet: The Confederacy's Most Controversial Soldier—A Biography* (New York: Simon & Schuster, 1993), 244–245.

98. Allan, "Memoranda," 15.

99. *OR,* 27/3:890, 896.

100. Ibid., 27/2:357–363. In his report, Longstreet states that he received these orders on June 20, but Lee's response to the changed line of march of the First Corps is dated June 17.

101. *OR,* 27/3:900.

102. James I. Robertson Jr., *General A. P. Hill: The Story of a Confederate Warrior* (New York: Random House, 1992), 205–206.

103. Quoted in ibid., 206.

104. Ibid., 207.

105. Heth, *Memoirs,* 175.

106. Ibid., 175.

107. Henry Kyd Douglas, *I Rode with Stonewall: Being Chiefly the War Experiences of the Youngest Member of Jackson's Staff from the John Brown Raid to the Hanging of Mrs. Surratt* (Atlanta, Ga.: Mockingbird Books, 1961), 239.

108. Ibid.

109. Ibid.

110. Freeman, *Lee's Lieutenants,* 3:94.

111. *OR,* 27/2:439–452.

112. Ibid., 313–325.

113. Robertson, *Hill,* 213.

114. *OR,* 27/2:305–311.

115. Freeman, *Lee's Lieutenants,* 3:101–105.

116. Marshall, *Aide-de-Camp,* 233; Raphael J. Moses autobiography, 1892, 82, Southern Historical Collection, Davis Library, University of North Carolina, Chapel Hill. Jefferson Davis offered, in a very indirect fashion, a degree of support for Longstreet's argument for the adoption of the tactical defensive. Davis wrote: "Had General Lee been able to compel the enemy to attack him in position, I think we should have had a complete victory." See Davis, *Rise and Fall,* 2:377.

117. Longstreet, *From Manassas to Appomattox,* 362.

118. Allan, "Memoranda," 14.

119. Walter H. Taylor, *General Lee: His Campaigns in Virginia, 1861–1865* (Lincoln: University of Nebraska Press, 1994), 203; Long, *Memoirs,* 281.

120. Longstreet, *From Manassas to Appomattox,* 362–368.

121. G. Moxley Sorrel, *Recollections of a Confederate Staff Officer* (New York: W. S. Konecky, 1994), 166–167. See also Edward Porter Alexander, *Fighting for the Confederacy: The Personal Recollections of General Edward Porter Alexander,* ed. Gary W. Gallagher (Chapel Hill: University of North Carolina Press, 1989), 237.

122. Wert, *Longstreet,* 268.

123. R. Lockwood Tower, ed. *Lee's Adjutant: The Wartime Letters of Colonel Walter Herron Taylor, 1862–1865* (Columbia: University of South Carolina Press, 1995), 61–63.

124. Fox, *Regimental Losses*, 541, 550.

125. Dowdey and Manarin, *The Wartime Papers of R. E. Lee*, 547–548.

126. Ibid., 551.

——— 3. The Bristoe Station Campaign ———

1. Lee began his invasion with a force of about 77,000 men in early June. See Edwin B. Coddington, *The Gettysburg Campaign: A Study in Command* (New York: Scribner's, 1968), 249. The official returns of the Army of Northern Virginia list the total casualties suffered at Gettysburg as 20,451, including 5,150 men captured. But Federal records list the names of 12,227 captured Confederates. See *OR*, 27/2:346. For this reason, and other discrepancies in the Confederate records, Coddington, *The Gettysburg Campaign*, 808n, suggested that Lee's casualties were even higher than he admitted, or at least reported. Including losses suffered during the march north and the retreat south, casualties certainly numbered about 25,000, or a third of Lee's army. By contrast, Lieutenant General John C. Pemberton surrendered about 20,000 at Vicksburg.

2. In a diary entry of July 26, 1863, Robert Garlick Hill Kean, Head of the Bureau of War, one of the divisions of the Confederate War Department, noted:

> Gettysburg has shaken my faith in Lee as a general. To fight an enemy superior in numbers at such terrible disadvantage of position in the heart of his own territory, when the freedom of movement gave him the advantage of selecting his own time and place for accepting battle, seems to have been a great military blunder. The battle . . . was the worst disaster that has ever befallen our arms—the loss of 15,000 to 20,000 men and all the prestige of the Army of Northern Virginia. This last is an immense loss; the former cannot be replaced.

See Kean, *Inside the Confederate Government: The Diary of Robert Garlick Hill Kean*, ed. Edward Younger (New York: Oxford University Press, 1957), 84. The men, of course, could not, and would not, be replaced! When Kean learned other details of the battle, he amended his entry, and blamed Lee's cavalry commander, Major General J. E. B. "Jeb" Stuart, for failing to keep Lee informed as to the enemy's whereabouts. Nevertheless, in an August 13, 1863, entry, written in possession of Lee's July 31 report on the campaign,

Kean wrote: "General Lee's report . . . is as jejeune and unsatisfactory a document as I ever read. The facts stand broadly out that, as at Sharpsburg, the enemy were more vigorous than he calculated and were amongst his troops before he was aware of their near approach." Kean then discussed Stuart's mishandling of the cavalry. The diarist concluded: "Hence a battle was fought without due concentration or preparation, and at a time and place, when and whereas General Lee says he had not proposed to deliver one." Ibid., 94.

3. Douglas Southall Freeman, *R. E. Lee: A Biography*, 4 vols. (New York: Scribner's, 1935), 3:145–146. The increase in morale was helped along by a "surge of religious fervor"; see William W. Hassler, *A. P. Hill: Lee's Forgotten General* (Richmond, Va.: Garrett & Massie, 1957), 172.

4. Steven E. Woodworth, *Davis and Lee at War* (Lawrence: University of Kansas Press, 1995), 253–254, and Douglas Southall Freeman, *Lee's Lieutenants: A Study in Command*, 3 vols. (New York: Scribner's, 1943), 3:217, address the problems caused by the "mass desertions" that occurred after Gettysburg. On August 10, 1863, the Army of Northern Virginia's returns list the total strength of the army as 68,104, whereas the strength of the army (before Longstreet's detachment) on August 31, 1863, was 56,326. To get some idea of the scale of the desertions, see *OR*, 27/2:636, 681, 764. Lee's army lost 17 percent of its manpower in three weeks! The desertions reversed over the next month and corps strength grew, but slowly. For details of the problem in Lieutenant General Ambrose Powell Hill's Third Corps, see James I. Robertson Jr., *General A. P. Hill: The Story of a Confederate Warrior* (New York: Random House, 1992), 232. In one of Hill's brigades, nine deserters were executed in September 1863.

5. One Confederate soldier, P. J. Coghill, wrote to his mother from Orange Court House on August 24, 1863, expressing his hope that the army would have a spell of "quiet," lamenting the fact that suddenly the Yankees seemed to be "getting the best of all the battles that is fought," and admitting "there is one thing our Soldiers are doing and that is deserting." James O. Coghill Papers, Perkins Library, Special Collections, Duke University, Durham, N.C. With regard to logistical problems, the Confederate railroad system was wearing down under the pressures of the war. In a July 28, 1863 letter to Lee, President Jefferson Davis admitted the problems of supplying the Army of Northern Virginia, stating "The railroads are growing worse." *OR*, 51/2:741–742.

6. Freeman, *Lee*, 3:162–163.

7. *OR*, 51/2:752–773. Frank Mills, a North Carolina soldier, wrote to his brother: "There is talk of Gen Lee rezining and quiting sirvis. . . . There is one thing sirtin. There must be a change of sum sort and that before long."

Frank Mills to H. M. Mills, August 6, 1863, Hugh Harrison Mills Collection, Correspondence, 1863–1865, #357.2.c., Joyner Library, Manuscript Division, East Carolina University, Greenville, N.C.

8. J. B. Jones, *A Rebel War Clerk's Diary: At the Confederate States Capital,* ed. Howard Swiggett, 2 vols. (New York: Old Hickory Bookshop, 1935), 1:380.

9. *OR,* 27/2:639–640.

10. James Longstreet, *From Manassas to Appomattox: Memoirs of the Civil War in America* (1896; reprint, New York: Mallard Press, 1991), 434; Freeman, *Lee's Lieutenants,* 3:221; Jeffrey D. Wert, *General James Longstreet: The Confederacy's Most Controversial Soldier—A Biography* (New York: Simon & Schuster, 1993), 300–303. Longstreet, as already noted, had proposed shifting troops between theaters to Secretary Seddon in May 1863, suggesting that the two divisions of his corps then detached from Lee's army be sent west to help mount a relief drive toward Vicksburg, rather than north to rejoin the Army of Northern Virginia. Lee had avoided those detachments by convincing Davis, Seddon, the cabinet, and ultimately even Longstreet, of the wisdom of an offensive in Virginia. Longstreet, *From Manassas to Appomattox,* 327–328; Freeman, *Lee's Lieutenants,* 3:221.

11. Freeman, *Lee,* 3:163–168.

12. Thomas L. Connelly and Archer Jones, *The Politics of Command: Factions and Ideas in Confederate Strategy* (Baton Rouge: Louisiana State University Press, 1973), 193.

13. Richard E. Beringer, Herman Hattaway, Archer Jones, and William N. Still Jr., *Why the South Lost the Civil War* (Athens: University of Georgia Press, 1986), 301.

14. Woodworth, *Davis and Lee at War,* 255–256.

15. Lee's preliminary report of July 31 concerning the Gettysburg campaign said nothing about "relieving the pressure" on the West. Lee instead stated that he had hoped "possibly, to draw to [the Army of the Potomac's] support troops designed to operate against other parts of the country." *OR,* 27/2:305. In Lee's final, more detailed report submitted in January 1864, he failed to even mention that the need to draw off troops from the West had been one of the objectives of the campaign. Ibid., 313.

16. Jones, *A Rebel War Clerk's Diary,* 2:28.

17. Longstreet, *From Manassas to Appomattox,* 435.

18. *OR,* 29/2:693. See also Longstreet's September 5, 1863, letter to Lee again arguing against a move in the East.

19. Henry McGilbert Wagstaff, ed., "Letters of Thomas Jackson Strayhorn," *North Carolina Historical Review* 13 (October 1936): 313.

20. Frank Mills to H. M. Mills, August 6, 1863.

21. Jones, *A Rebel War Clerk's Diary*, 2:32.

22. Freeman, *Lee*, 3:165–166; *OR*, 29/2:700–701.

23. Ibid. Lee also advised Davis that a new army commander, if one were to be chosen to succeed Bragg, ought to be picked from among those officers already in the western theater. Lee's recommendation undermined whatever chances Longstreet had of being given overall command, thereby increasing the chance that he would return, with his troops, to Virginia. Emory M. Thomas, *Robert E. Lee: A Biography* (New York: W. W. Norton, 1995), 289–290, pointed out that Longstreet, during his short interlude of independent command near Suffolk, Virginia, in the spring of 1863, failed to impress Lee, and may not have been as well suited as many historians assume to high command. Such doubts about Longstreet's capacity help to explain why Lee was unwilling to endorse Longstreet as Bragg's replacement before Chickamauga, although it is hard to believe that Longstreet, whatever his weaknesses, would not have performed better than Bragg.

24. Jones, *A Rebel War Clerk's Diary*, 2:32, 36; and Kean, *Diary*, 103.

25. *OR*, 29/2:702.

26. Ibid., 636, 681, 764.

27. Major General George E. Pickett's division of the First Corps, numbering about four thousand, was still recovering from its disastrous assault at Gettysburg and did not accompany Longstreet to Tennessee. The division was sent instead to Richmond.

28. *OR*, 29/2:118.

29. Freeman, *Lee*, 3:168.

30. *OR*, 29/2:711–712.

31. Ibid., 738–739.

32. Ibid., 748, 750, 752.

33. Meade was preparing to launch an offensive when he received the order to send two corps west. See the account by Meade's chief of staff, Major General Andrew A. Humphreys, in *From Gettysburg to the Rapidan: The Army of the Potomac, July 1863 to April 1864* (New York: Scribner's, 1883), 11. One can doubt whether Meade's fall offensive would have carried his army to the gates of Richmond as Lee professed to believe.

34. Jones, *A Rebel War Clerk's Diary*, 2:58.

35. Ibid., 2:60. See also the October 4 entry in Kean, *Diary*, 106.

36. Humphreys, *From Gettysburg to the Rapidan*, 15, noted that Lee's instructions to Brigadier General John D. Imboden in the Shenandoah Valley to guard the gaps in the mountains on Lee's left suggests the possibility that he had more in mind than "merely to bring on an engagement at Culpeper Court House."

37. *OR*, 27/2:753–754. Thomas, *Lee*, 310, notes that Lee "began immediately to seek an opportunity for offensive action" when he learned of the detachments from Meade's army.

38. *OR*, 27/2:780.

39. Ibid., 27/1:406. In an October 19 letter to the quartermaster general, Brigadier General Alexander R. Lawton, Lee lamented the fact that he had failed to throw Meade back across the Potomac. Ibid., 27/2:794.

40. Ibid., 27/1:406. See memoir of Samuel D. Buck, 78, Samuel D. Buck Papers, Perkins Library, Special Collections, Duke University, Durham, N.C. The manuscript was published as Samuel D. Buck, *With the Old Confeds: Actual Experiences of a Captain in the Line* (Baltimore: H. E. Houck, 1925).

41. *OR*, 27/1:407, 410–411.

42. Ibid., 410–411.

43. Walter H. Taylor, *Four Years with General Lee* (Bloomington: Indiana University Press, 1962), 115.

44. Jubal Anderson Early, *War Memoirs: Autobiographical Sketch and Narrative of the War Between the States* (1912; reprint, Bloomington: Indiana University Press, 1960), 303.

45. Hassler, *A. P. Hill*, 175.

46. James D. McCabe Jr., *Life and Campaigns of General Robert E. Lee* (Atlanta, Ga.: National Publication, 1870), 415.

47. Shelby Foote, *The Civil War: A Narrative*, 3 vols. (New York: Random House, 1958–1974), 2:786. Other accounts that suggest Lee wanted to bring on a battle include Clement A. Evans, ed., *Confederate Military History*, 12 vols. (Atlanta, Ga.: Confederate Publishing, 1899), 3:425–426; Fitzhugh Lee, *General Lee* (New York: D. Appleton, 1895), 315; and L. VanLoan Naisawald, "The Battle of Bristoe Station," *Virginia Cavalcade* 18 (Autumn 1968): 40.

48. Robertson, *Hill*, 232.

49. Thomas, *Lee*, 310.

50. Freeman, *Lee*, 3:170.

51. *OR*, 27/1:406.

52. Ibid., 407.

53. Ibid., 27/2:624.

54. Two corps totaling about 14,000 men were sent west, but the remaining corps were reinforced in a process continuing since Gettysburg. For example, the First Corps, bloodied at Gettysburg, had 9,985 men on August 31; on 31 October, it had 13,819 men, an increase of 38 percent.

55. I am at a loss to determine how James Robertson concluded that the detachment of the Federal Eleventh and Twelfth corps brought Lee's

strength "almost to numerical equality" with that of Meade. See Robertson, *Hill*, 232.

56. *OR*, 27/2:757–758; 51/2:772.

57. *OR*, 27/2:773.

58. Jones, *A Rebel War Clerk's Diary*, 2:66, 70.

59. *OR*, 27/1:769.

60. Ibid., 406, 407.

61. Ibid., 406.

62. John Cheeves Haskell, a South Carolina artilleryman serving with Lee, considered the Army of Northern Virginia at the time of the campaign: "A demoralized army and for this, I hold General Lee largely responsible." See "Memoir of John Cheeves Haskell," 37, John Cheeves Haskell Papers, Perkins Library, Special Collections, Duke University, Durham, N.C.

63. Freeman, *Lee*, 3:170; Thomas, *Lee*, 310.

64. Robertson, in his sympathetic though critical biography *Hill*, 194, notes that Hill "would never quite master that transition" from division to corps commander gained in the reorganization of the Army of Northern Virginia after Chancellorsville. John Cheeves Haskell wrote of Hill: "General Hill was eccentric to the verge of wrongheadedness." See Haskell, "Memoir," 30.

65. Freeman, *Lee*, 3:170–171. Regarding pay, Lee wrote Davis on October 3 that if it were "at all possible, I should like to have the men paid regularly." *OR*, 29/2:769. The men of the Sixth North Carolina Regiment had not been paid for five months and a quarter of the men "were without blankets, coats or pants." See Richard W. Iobst and Louis H. Manarin, *The Bloody Sixth: The Sixth North Carolina Regiment, Confederate States of America* (Raleigh, N.C.: North Carolina Confederate Centennial Commission, 1965), 153.

66. *OR*, 27/1:408–409. Lee earlier wrote Seddon and Davis in letters dated October 15 and 16: "The men are poorly provided with clothes, shoes, blankets, and overcoats, and I am unwilling to subject them to the suffering that might ensue." Ibid., 407. The same passage appears in both letters.

67. Freeman, *Lee*, 3:184.

68. Lawton acknowledged the receipt of Lee's "recent letter." See *OR*, 27/2:784–785.

69. Freeman, *Lee*, 3:171.

70. Coddington, *The Gettysburg Campaign*, 6.

71. *OR*, 27/2:158, 179–180.

72. Kean, *Diary*, 85. Emphasis in the original.

73. *OR*, 29/2:771–772. See also Woodworth, *Davis and Lee at War*, 258.

74. *OR*, 27/2:780.

75. Ibid., 782.

76. Ibid., 29/1:405–406. My emphasis.

77. Ibid., 410.

78. *OR*, 27/2:778, 779, 780, 782. Lee's letters of October 9–11 are not datelined Orange Court-House, as they had been before the offensive began.

79. Freeman, *Lee*, 3:171. Freeman cites Lee's October 11 letter to Seddon, which mentions the press leaks, as support for his contention that Lee recognized that secrecy had been lost. Yet Freeman makes no mention of the fact that in the same letter, Lee denied to the secretary of war that the army had passed the Rapidan, when, in fact, it had two days before. Ibid., 172.

80. *OR*, 29/2:790.

81. The Confederate correspondence for the month of September 1863 that appears in *OR*, 29/2 is replete with these letters.

82. Ibid., 702–703.

83. Ibid., 777.

84. Ibid., 29/1:408–409. Seddon, in a letter dated October 16, had laid out the problems facing the Confederacy on a number of fronts, despite the victory at Chickamauga. Lee doubted the wisdom of many of Seddon's suggested countermoves. Despite Lee's worst fears, the lateness of the season, Meade's end-of-November Mine Run offensive, and the weakness of the Army of Northern Virginia after the failed Bristoe Station campaign ensured that Lee did not have to make significant detachments from his army. Brigadier General Robert F. Hoke's shattered brigade went to coastal North Carolina, but Lee resisted other detachments, as well as efforts on the part of state authorities in Texas and Florida to recall their troops. Lee also dodged yet another effort by Davis to convince Lee to go west to take command from Bragg. While Lee did not reject the proposal, he displayed his usual lack of enthusiasm, arguing as well that he would not receive cooperation in the West and that his senior corps commander, Ewell, was too ill to take over command of the Army of Northern Virginia. (Jubal Early had, in fact, commanded the Second Corps during the Mine Run campaign because of Ewell's illness.) See ibid., 29/2:861.

85. Ibid., 29/2:780. My emphasis.

86. Ibid., 242.

87. William D. Henderson, *The Road to Bristoe Station: Campaigning with Lee and Meade, August 1–October 20, 1863* (Lynchburg, Va.: H. E. Howard, 1987).

88. *OR*, 29/2:245.

89. Ibid., 244–245.

90. See assorted Confederate reports printed in *OR*, 29/1:417–419.

91. *OR*, 29/2:266. See also Martin T. McMahon, "From Gettysburg to the Coming of Grant," in *Battles and Leaders of the Civil War*, ed. Robert Underwood Johnson and Clarence Clough Buel, 4 vols. (Secaucus, N.J.: Castle, n.d.), 4:83.

92. *OR*, 29/2:252.

93. Ibid., 263.

94. Details of Meade's thinking and movements can be found in Freeman Cleaves, *Meade of Gettysburg* (Norman: University of Oklahoma Press, 1960), 196–200; and in Meade's December 6, 1863, report on the campaign, which appears in *OR*, 29/1:8–11.

95. Humphreys, *From Gettysburg to the Rapidan*, 18.

96. Ibid., 20. Of interest is Humphreys's admission that he and Meade discussed the possibility of taking up a position near Manassas but rejected the idea "because of the former operations there." Clearly, not only the minds of the Confederates were flashing back to the battles fought near Bull Run. The decision to retire, for psychological, rather than military reasons, to a position further to the north near Centreville may have saved Lee from suffering a larger defeat at Bristoe since the main body of Meade's army was too far away to take full advantage of Hill's distress. See ibid., 21–22.

97. Freeman, *Lee's Lieutenants*, 240.

98. James A. Graham, "Twenty-seventh Regiment," in *Histories of the Several Regiments and Battalions from North Carolina in the Great War, 1861–1865*, ed. Walter Clark, 5 vols. (Goldsboro, N.C.: Nash Brothers, 1901), 2:440.

99. Freeman, *Lee's Lieutenants*, 241; Foote, *The Civil War*, 2:786. Years after Bristoe Station, that spirit continued to inspire Captain Buck of the Thirteenth Virginia Infantry, who wrote: "Only half an hour sooner would have put us in a position to have captured Warren's Corps and ten minutes would have saved Hill's men, or at least have met the enemy in the open field, and that meant whipping him." Buck memoir manuscript, 79.

100. *OR*, 29/1:439–453.

101. Burke Davis, *Jeb Stuart: The Last Cavalier* (New York: Rinehart, 1957), 363.

102. Diary of the Bristoe Station Campaign, Richard Stoddert Ewell letterbook, Perkins Library, Special Collections, Duke University, Durham, N.C.

103. Ibid.

104. *OR*, 29/1:426–427.

105. Ibid., 462–464.

106. Ibid., 474–475.

107. For a secondary account written from Hill's perspective, see Robertson, *Hill*, 234–240.

108. See Heth's report, *OR*, 29/1:430–432. Dick Anderson, another of Hill's division commanders, termed the Federal troops "a column." Ibid., 428–429.

109. Heth's report, ibid., 430–432; Graham, "Twenty-seventh Regiment," 441. Emphasis in the original.

110. Graham, "Twenty-seventh Regiment," 441.

111. Warren's report in *OR*, 29/1:234–247.

112. Ibid., 426–427.

113. Ibid., 434–436.

114. H. C. Kearney, "Fifteenth Regiment," in Clark, *North Carolina Regiments*, 1:743.

115. Henry McGilbert Wagstaff, ed., "The James A. Graham Papers, 1861–1864," in *James Sprunt Historical Studies*, vol. 20 (Chapel Hill: University of North Carolina Press, 1928), 157.

116. W. J. Martin and E. R. Outlaw, "Eleventh Regiment," ibid., 593.

117. Freeman, *Lee's Lieutenants*, 3:245.

118. Graham, "Twenty-seventh Regiment," 443.

119. According to Humphreys, *From Gettysburg to the Rapidan*, 29, Warren actually had only about three thousand men on hand when he repulsed Hill's attack. Hill commanded nearly five times that number; he had no need to wait for Ewell to come up, and ought to have been able to drive Warren from the field had the divisions of the Third Corps been better handled.

120. Ewell, *Diary of the Bristoe Station Campaign*.

121. Freeman, *Lee's Lieutenants*, 3:247.

122. Quoted in J. F. C. Fuller, *Grant and Lee: A Study in Generalship* (New York: Scribner's, 1933), 127.

123. For contemporary criticism of Hill, see Robertson, *Hill*, 239.

124. *OR*, 29/1:410–411.

125. Ibid., 427. Many of the North Carolinians involved at Bristoe—and both Cooke's and Kirkland's Brigades were from North Carolina—blamed Hill for the debacle. Leander Gwynn Hunt, the assistant surgeon of the Twenty-seventh North Carolina, wrote his father: "I saw the whole fight. . . . We had only two Brigs engaged they had two *Corps*. . . . We had plenty of troops near at hand but had no support. *Someone is to blame.* I dont know who it is without we put it on A. P. Hill." Hunt letter, October 21, 1863, Grimes-Bryan Papers, Correspondence, 1860–1863, #16.1.c, East Carolina University Library, Manuscript Division, Greenville, N.C.

126. Quoted in G. F. R. Henderson, *Stonewall Jackson and the American Civil War* (New York: Da Capo, 1988), 477.

127. Robertson, *Hill*, 240, notes that it was clear that after Bristoe Station Hill "was no longer the spirited, hard-driving man who had carried the Light Division to fame." According to Robertson, "Hill lacked the

breadth of vision and wisdom to be superb at the head of a corps. . . . Hill simply did not—or could not—adjust as well to the next step up the military ladder."

128. R. Lockwood Tower, ed., *Lee's Adjutant: The Wartime Letters of Colonel Walter Herron Taylor, 1862–1865* (Columbia: University of South Carolina Press, 1995), 75–78. Emphasis in the original.

129. Letter, November 1, 1863, Leander Gwynn Hunt Papers, Joyner Library, Manuscripts Division, East Carolina University, Greenville, N.C.

130. Tower, *Taylor Letters*, 75–78.

131. Freeman, *Lee*, 3:181.

132. Ibid.

133. *OR*, 29/1 does not contain a copy of a report from Ewell on the Bristoe Station campaign.

134. See the letter of Leonidas Spencer (2:00 P.M.) of October 20, 1863, Joyner Family Papers, Southern Historical Collection, Davis Library, University of North Carolina, Chapel Hill; the report of Federal colonel John Fraser (2:30 P.M.), *OR*, 29/1:260; and James A. Graham (3:00 P.M.), in Wagstaff, "The James A. Graham Papers, 1861–1864," 157.

135. Freeman, *Lee*, 3:170; 4:521–525.

136. Tower, *Taylor Letters*, 74–75.

137. *OR*, 29/1:610–611.

138. See Freeman, *Lee*, 3:188.

139. Robert E. Lee Jr., *Recollections and Letters of General Robert E. Lee* (Garden City, N.Y.: Doubleday, Page, 1924), 111.

140. For Early's report, see *OR*, 29/1:618–626. See also Early, *Memoirs*, 307–325.

141. Hoke had been detached to North Carolina with some of his men to round up deserters, and in his absence Colonel Archibald C. Godwin commanded the remainder of the brigade. See Iobst and Manarin, *The Bloody Sixth*, 151. See also Humphreys, *From Gettysburg to the Rapidan*, 37–46.

142. Tower, *Taylor Letters*, 82–83.

143. See Freeman, *Lee*, 3:264–269; Cleaves, *Meade*, 203–204.

144. Neill W. Ray, "Sixth Regiment," in Clark, *North Carolina Regiments*, 1:319.

145. Ibid., 1:320.

146. Haskell memoir, 41.

147. Kean, *Diary*, 114.

148. Ibid., 121–122.

149. Fuller, *Grant and Lee*, 263. Emphasis in the original.

150. Tower, *Taylor Letters*, 78–80. For soldiers' expectations that they would now be sent west, see William "Bud" Hunt (Twenty-seventh North Carolina Infantry), letter, October 26, 1863, Brian Grimes Papers, Joyner Library, Manuscript Division, East Carolina University, Greenville, N.C. He wrote: "There is some Probability of our going west before long." J. D. Joyner, of the Seventh North Carolina Infantry, wrote his mother on October 19 that "it is talked and believed by officers high in authority that our troops will be sent to the west in a few days." See Joyner Family Papers, Southern Historical Collection, Davis Library, University of North Carolina, Chapel Hill. On October 17, 1863, John Andrew Ramsay wrote his cousin of the failure at Bristoe Station and likewise concluded that if Lee did not keep going north, "one corps of this army will go to Bragg." John Andrew Ramsay Papers, Southern Historical Collection, Davis Library, University of North Carolina, Chapel Hill.

—— Conclusions ——

1. Jubal A. Early, "The Campaigns of Gen. Robert E. Lee. An Address by Lieut. General Jubal A. Early, before Washington and Lee University, January 19, 1872," in Gary W. Gallagher, ed., *Lee: The Soldier* (Lincoln: University of Nebraska Press, 1996), 65.

2. Russell F. Weigley, *The American Way of War: A History of United States Military Strategy and Policy* (New York: Macmillan, 1973), 127.

3. Early, "The Campaigns of Robert E. Lee," 67.

4. For example, see Russell F. Weigley, "American Strategy from Its Beginnings through the First World War," in *Makers of Modern Strategy: From Machiavelli to the Nuclear Age*, ed. Peter Paret (Princeton, N.J.: Princeton University Press, 1986). Paddy Griffith, in *Battle Tactics of the Civil War* (New Haven, Conn.: Yale University Press, 1989), offered a provocative and, to this author, convincing argument that, in fact, Napoleonic tactics were still applicable in the American Civil War for myriad reasons: among them the limited ammunition supplies of individual soldiers and slower rates of fire which ensured that engagement ranges remained about what they had been during the wars of the French Revolution and Empire. For a good synopsis of what can be termed the traditional view of Civil War weaponry and tactics, see Grady McWhiney and Perry D. Jamieson, *Attack and Die: Civil War Military Tactics and the Southern Heritage* (University: University of Alabama Press, 1982).

5. Carl von Clausewitz, *On War*, trans. and ed. Michael Howard and Peter Paret (Princeton, N.J.: Princeton University Press, 1984), 75. Emphasis in the original.

6. Ibid., 258.

7. Ibid., book 8.

8. Gordon A. Craig, "Delbrück: The Military Historian," in *Makers of Modern Strategy: Military Thought from Machiavelli to Hitler*, ed. Edward Mead Earle (Princeton, N.J.: Princeton University Press, 1943), 260–283.

9. Hans Delbrück, *History of the Art of War*, trans. Walter J. Renfroe Jr., 4 vols. (Lincoln: University of Nebraska Press, 1990), 4:294. My emphasis.

10. Steven E. Woodworth, *Davis and Lee at War* (Lawrence: University of Kansas Press, 1995), 157.

11. Richard E. Beringer, Herman Hattaway, Archer Jones, and William N. Still Jr., *Why the South Lost the Civil War* (Athens: University of Georgia Press, 1986), 439.

12. Gary W. Gallagher, "Another Look at the Generalship of R. E. Lee," in Gallagher, *Lee*, 275–286.

13. Clausewitz, *On War*, 526.

14. Robert Debs Heinl Jr., ed., *Dictionary of Military and Naval Quotations* (Annapolis, Md.: United States Naval Institute, 1966), 239.

15. J. F. C. Fuller, *Grant and Lee: A Study in Personality and Generalship* (New York: Scribner's, 1933), 125. Compare, for example, Lee's spasmodic correspondence about supply problems with a remark attributed to the Duke of Wellington during the Peninsula campaign: "It is very necessary to attend to all this detail and to trace a biscuit from Lisbon into a man's mouth on the frontier and to provide for its removal from place to place by land or by water, or no military operations can be carried out." Quoted in Heinl, *Dictionary of Military and Naval Quotations*, 175.

16. Walter H. Taylor, *Four Years with General Lee* (Bloomington: Indiana University Press, 1962), 77.

17. Clausewitz, *On War*, 140.

18. Robert E. Lee Jr., *Recollections and Letters of General Robert E. Lee* (Garden City, N.Y.: Doubleday, Page, 1924), 95.

19. David G. Chandler, *The Campaigns of Napoleon* (New York: Macmillan, 1966), 384–387.

20. For a good discussion of Jomini, see John Shy, "Jomini," in Paret, *Makers of Modern Strategy*, 143–185.

21. K. Jack Bauer, *The Mexican War, 1846–1848* (New York: Macmillan, 1974), 232–236.

22. Weigley, "American Strategy," 426; Douglas Southall Freeman, *R. E. Lee: A Biography*, 4 vols. (New York: Scribner's, 1935), 1:218–220, 237.

23. Freeman, *Lee*, 1:242.

24. Jubal Anderson Early, *War Memoirs: Autobiographical Sketch and Narrative of the War Between the States* (1912; reprint, Bloomington: Indiana University Press, 1960), 316.

25. Fuller, *Grant and Lee*, 126.

26. William Shakespeare, *Henry V*, ii, 4.

27. G. F. R. Henderson, *Stonewall Jackson and the American Civil War* (New York: Da Capo, 1988), 477.

Bibliography

Primary Sources

Manuscripts

Joyner Library, East Carolina University, Manuscript Division, Greenville, N.C.
  Brian Grimes Papers
  Grimes-Bryan Papers
  Leander Gwynn Hunt Papers
  Hugh Harrison Mills Collection
Perkins Library, Special Collections, Duke University, Durham, N.C.
  Samuel D. Buck Papers
  James O. Coghill Papers
  Confederate States of America Archives, Army Units, North Carolina Regiments
  A. J. Dula Papers
  Benjamin and Richard Stoddert Ewell, Richard Stoddert Ewell letterbook
  John Cheeves Haskell Papers
Southern Historical Collection, Davis Library, University of North Carolina, Chapel Hill
  Berry Greenwood Papers
  Joyner Family Papers
  Raphael J. Moses Autobiography
  Abram David Pollock Papers
  John Andrew Ramsay Papers
  George E. Waller Papers

Published Papers and Letters

Dowdey, Clifford, and Louis H. Manarin, eds. *The Wartime Papers of R. E. Lee.* Boston: Little, Brown, 1961.

Ewell, Richard Stoddert. *The Making of a Soldier: Letters of General R. S. Ewell.* Edited by Percy Gatling Hamlin. Richmond, Va.: Whittet & Shepperson, 1935.

Nelson, Horatio. *The Dispatches and Letters of Vice Admiral Lord Nelson.* Edited by Nicholas Harris Nicolas. 7 vols. London: H. Colburn, 1845.

Sears, Stephen W., ed. *The Civil War Papers of George B. McClellan: Selected Correspondence, 1860–1865.* New York: Ticknor & Fields, 1989.

Tower, R. Lockwood, ed. *Lee's Adjutant: The Wartime Letters of Colonel Walter Herron Taylor, 1862–1865.* Columbia: University of South Carolina Press, 1995.

U.S. War Department. *The War of the Rebellion: A Compilation of the Official Records of the Union and Confederate Armies.* 128 vols. in four series. Washington, D.C.: Government Printing Office, 1880–1901. In addition to the printed edition, I also used the CD-ROM version. Carmel, Ind.: Guild Press of Indiana, Inc., 1996.

Memoirs and Diaries

Alexander, Edward Porter. *Fighting for the Confederacy: The Personal Recollections of General Edward Porter Alexander.* Edited by Gary W. Gallagher. Chapel Hill: The University of North Carolina Press, 1989.

Blackford, W. W. *War Years with Jeb Stuart.* New York: Scribner's, 1945.

Buck, Samuel D. *With the Old Confeds: Actual Experiences of a Captain in the Line.* Baltimore: H. E. Houck, 1925.

Davis, Jefferson. *The Rise and Fall of the Confederate Government.* 2 vols. Richmond, Va.: Garrett & Massie, n.d.

DeLeon, T. C. *Four Years in Rebel Capitals: An Inside View of Life in the Southern Confederacy, From Birth to Death.* Mobile, Ala.: Gossip Printing, 1890.

Douglas, Henry Kyd. *I Rode with Stonewall: Being Chiefly the War Experiences of the Youngest Member of Jackson's Staff from the John Brown Raid to the Hanging of Mrs. Surratt.* Atlanta, Ga.: Mockingbird Books, 1961.

Early, Jubal Anderson. *War Memoirs: Autobiographical Sketch and Narrative of the War Between the States.* 1912. Reprint, Bloomington: Indiana University Press, 1960.

Fremantle, Arthur James Lyon. *The Fremantle Diary: Being the Journal of Lieutenant Colonel Arthur James Lyon Fremantle, Coldstream Guards, on His Three Months in the Southern States.* Edited by Walter Lord. Boston: Little, Brown, 1954.

Gordon, John B. *Reminiscences of the Civil War.* Baton Rouge: Louisiana State University Press, 1993.

Heth, Henry. *The Memoirs of Henry Heth.* Edited by James L. Morrison Jr. Westport, Conn.: Greenwood Press, 1974.

Hotchkiss, Jedediah. *Make Me a Map of the Valley: The Civil War Journal of Stonewall Jackson's Topographer.* Edited by Archie P. McDonald. Dallas: Southern Methodist University Press, 1973.

Humphreys, Andrew A. *From Gettysburg to the Rapidan: The Army of the Potomac, July 1863 to April 1864.* New York: Scribner's, 1883.

Jones, J. B. *A Rebel War Clerk's Diary: At the Confederate States Capital.* Edited by Howard Swiggett. 2 vols. New York: Old Hickory Bookshop, 1935.

Kean, Robert Garlick Hill. *Inside the Confederate Government: The Diary of Robert Garlick Hill Kean.* Edited by Edward Younger. New York: Oxford University Press, 1957.

Long, A. L. *Memoirs of Robert E. Lee: His Military and Personal History.* Edison, N.J.: Blue & Grey Press, 1983.

McClendan, William Augustus. *Recollections of War Times by an Old Veteran While under Stonewall Jackson and Lieutenant General James Longstreet, How I Got In, and How I Got Out.* Montgomery, Ala.: Paragon Press, 1909.

Marshall, Charles. *An Aide-de-Camp of Lee: Being the Papers of Colonel Charles Marshall, Sometime Aide-de-Camp, Military Secretary, and Assistant Adjutant-General on the Staff of Robert E. Lee, 1862–1865.* Edited by Sir Frederick Maurice. Boston: Little, Brown, 1927.

Reagan, John H. *Memoirs: With Special Reference to Secession and the Civil War.* Edited by Walter Flavius McCales. New York and Washington, D.C.: Neale Publishing, 1906.

Sorrel, G. Moxley. *Recollections of a Confederate Staff Officer.* New York: W. S. Konecky, 1994.

Taylor, Walter H. *Four Years with General Lee.* Bloomington: Indiana University Press, 1962.

Von Borcke, Heros. *Memoirs of the Confederate War for Independence.* 2 vols. New York: Peter Smith, 1938.

⸺ Secondary Sources ⸺

Books

Bauer, K. Jack. *The Mexican War, 1846–1848.* New York: Macmillan, 1974.

Beringer, Richard E., Herman Hattaway, Archer Jones, and William N. Still Jr. *Why the South Lost the Civil War.* Athens: University of Georgia Press, 1986.

Bridges, Hal. *Lee's Maverick General: Daniel Harvey Hill.* Lincoln: University of Nebraska Press, 1991.

Chandler, David G. *The Campaigns of Napoleon.* New York: Macmillan, 1966.

Clark, Walter, ed. *Histories of the Several Regiments and Battalions from North Carolina in the Great War, 1861–1865.* 5 vols. Goldsboro, N.C.: Nash Brothers, 1901.

Clausewitz, Carl von. *On War.* Translated and edited by Michael Howard and Peter Paret. Princeton: N.J.: Princeton University Press, 1984.

Cleaves, Freeman. *Meade of Gettysburg.* Norman: University of Oklahoma Press, 1960.

Coddington, Edwin B. *The Gettysburg Campaign: A Study in Command.* New York: Scribner's, 1968.

Connelly, Thomas L. *The Marble Man: Robert E. Lee and His Image in American Society.* New York: Knopf, 1977.

Connelly, Thomas L., and Archer Jones. *The Politics of Command: Factions and Ideas in Confederate Strategy.* Baton Rouge: Louisiana State University Press, 1973.

Connelly, Thomas L., and Barbara L. Bellows. *God and General Longstreet: The Lost Cause and the Southern Mind.* Baton Rouge: Louisiana State University Press, 1982.

Craig, Gordon A. "Delbrück: The Military Historian." In *Makers of Modern Strategy: Military Thought from Machiavelli to Hitler,* edited by Edward Mead Earle. Princeton, N.J.: Princeton University Press, 1943.

Dabney, R. L. *Life and Campaigns of Lieut.-Gen. Thomas J. Jackson.* New York: Blecock, 1866.

Davis, Burke. *Jeb Stuart: The Last Cavalier.* New York: Rinehart, 1957.

Davis, William C. *Jefferson Davis: The Man and His Hour.* (New York: Harper-Collins, 1991.

Delbrück, Hans. *History of the Art of War.* Translated by Walter J. Renfroe Jr. 4 vols. Lincoln: University of Nebraska Press, 1990.

Dowdey, Clifford. *Lee.* New York: Bonanza Books, 1965.

Evans, Clement A., ed. *Confederate Military History.* 12 vols. Atlanta, Ga.: Confederate Publishing, 1899.

Foote, Shelby. *The Civil War: A Narrative.* 3 vols. New York: Random House, 1958–1974.

Fox, William F. *Regimental Losses In The American Civil War, 1861–1865: A Treatise On The Extent And Nature Of The Mortuary Losses In The Union Regiments, With Full And Exhaustive Statistics Compiled From The Official Records On File In The State Military Bureaus And At Washington.* Albany, N.Y.: Albany Publishing, 1889.

Freeman, Douglas Southall. *Lee's Lieutenants: A Study in Command.* 3 vols. New York: Scribner's, 1943.

————. *R. E. Lee: A Biography.* 4 vols. New York: Scribner's, 1935.

Fuller, J. F. C. *Grant and Lee: A Study in Personality and Generalship.* New York: Scribner's, 1933.

Gallagher, Gary W., ed. *Lee: The Soldier.* Lincoln: University of Nebraska Press, 1996.

Graham, James A. "Twenty-seventh Regiment." In *Histories of the Several Regiments and Battalions from North Carolina in the Great War, 1861–1865,* edited by Walter Clark. 5 vols. Goldsboro, N.C.: Nash Brothers, 1901.

Griffith, Paddy. *Battle Tactics of the Civil War.* New Haven, Conn.: Yale University Press, 1989.

Hamlin, Percy Gatling. *"Old Bald Head" (General R. S. Ewell): The Portrait of a Soldier.* Strasburg, Va.: Shenandoah Publishing House, 1940.

Hassler, Warren W., Jr. *General George B. McClellan: Shield of the Union.* Baton Rouge: Louisiana State University Press, 1957.

Hassler, William W. *A. P. Hill: Lee's Forgotten General.* Richmond, Va.: Garrett & Massie, 1957.

Heinl, Robert Debs, Jr., ed. *Dictionary of Military and Naval Quotations.* Annapolis, Md.: United States Naval Institute, 1966.

Henderson, G. F. R. *Stonewall Jackson and the American Civil War.* New York: DaCapo, 1988.

Henderson, William D. *The Road to Bristoe Station: Campaigning with Lee and Meade, August 1–October 20, 1863.* Lynchburg, Va.: H. E. Howard, 1987.

Hennessy, John H. *Return to Bull Run: The Campaign and Battle of Second Manassas.* New York: Simon & Schuster, 1993.

Iobst, Richard W., and Louis H. Manarin. *The Bloody Sixth: The Sixth North Carolina Regiment, Confederate States of America.* Raleigh, N.C.: North Carolina Confederate Centennial Commission, 1965.

Johnson, Robert Underwood, and Clarence Clough Buel, eds. *Battles and Leaders of the Civil War.* 4 vols. Secaucus, N.J.: Castle, n.d.

Jones, Archer. *Civil War Command and Strategy: The Process of Victory and Defeat.* New York: Free Press, 1992.

Jones, J. William. *Personal Reminiscences of General Robert E. Lee.* Baton Rouge: Louisiana State University Press, 1994.

Kearny. H. C. "Fifteenth Regiment." In *Histories of the Several Regiments and Battalions from North Carolina in the Great War, 1861–1865,* edited by Walter Clark. 5 vols. Goldsboro, N.C.: Nash Brothers, 1901.

Kegel, James A. *North with Lee and Jackson: The Lost Story of Gettysburg.* Mechanicsville, Pa.: Stackpole, 1996.

Lee, Fitzhugh. *General Lee.* New York: D. Appleton, 1895.

Lee, Robert E., Jr. *Recollections and Letters of General Robert E. Lee.* Garden City, N.Y.: Doubleday, Page, 1924.

Longford, Elizabeth. *Wellington: The Years of the Sword.* New York: Harper & Row, 1969.

Longstreet, James. *From Manassas to Appomattox: Memoirs of the Civil War in America.* 1896. Reprint, New York: Mallard Press, 1991.

McCabe, James D., Jr., *Life and Campaigns of General Robert E. Lee.* Atlanta, Ga.: National Publication, 1870.

McKenzie, John D. *Uncertain Glory: Lee's Generalship Re-Examined.* New York: Hippocrene, 1997.

McMahon, Martin T. "From Gettysburg to the Coming of Grant." In *Battles and Leaders of the Civil War,* edited by Robert Underwood Johnson and Clarence Clough Buel. 4 vols. Secaucus, N.J.: Castle, n.d.

McWhiney, Grady, and Perry D. Jamieson. *Attack and Die: Civil War Military Tactics and the Southern Heritage.* University: University of Alabama Press, 1982.

Napoléon I. *The Military Maxims of Napoleon.* Translated by George C. D'Aguilar. New York: Da Capo, 1995.

Nolan, Alan T. *Lee Considered: General Robert E. Lee and Civil War History.* Chapel Hill: University of North Carolina Press, 1991.

Paret, Peter, ed. *Makers of Modern Strategy: From Machiavelli to the Nuclear Age.* Princeton, N.J.: Princeton University Press, 1986.

Patrick, Rembert. *Jefferson Davis and His Cabinet.* Baton Rouge: Louisiana State University Press, 1944.

Procter, Ben H. *Not without Honor: The Life of John H. Reagan.* Austin: University of Texas Press, 1962.

Ray, Neill W. "Sixth Regiment." In *Histories of the Several Regiments and Battalions from North Carolina in the Great War, 1861–1865,* edited by Walter Clark. 5 vols. Goldsboro, N.C.: Nash Brothers, 1901.

Robertson, James I., Jr. *General A. P. Hill: The Story of a Confederate Warrior.* New York: Random House, 1992.

———. *Stonewall Jackson: The Man, the Soldier, the Legend.* New York: Macmillan, 1997.

Shy, John. "Jomini." In *Makers of Modern Strategy: From Machiavelli to the Nuclear Age,* edited by Peter Paret. Princeton, N.J.: Princeton University Press, 1986.

Taylor, Walter H. *General Lee: His Campaigns in Virginia, 1861–1865.* Lincoln: University of Nebraska Press, 1994).

Thomas, Emory M. *Robert E. Lee: A Biography.* New York: W. W. Norton, 1995.

Tucker, Glenn. *Lee and Longstreet at Gettysburg.* Indianapolis: xBobbs-Merrill, 1968.

Van Creveld, Martin. *Command in War.* Cambridge, Mass.: Harvard University Press, 1985.

Wagstaff, Henry McGilbert, ed. "The James A. Graham Papers, 1861–1864." In *James Sprunt Historical Studies.* Vol. 20. Chapel Hill: University of North Carolina Press, 1928.

Warner, Ezra J. *Generals in Gray: Lives of the Confederate Commanders.* Baton Rouge: Louisiana State University Press, 1959.

Weigley, Russell F. "American Strategy from Its Beginnings through the First World War." In *Makers of Modern Strategy: From Machiavelli to the Nuclear Age,* edited by Peter Paret. Princeton, N.J.: Princeton University Press, 1986.

———. *The American Way of War: A History of United States Military Strategy and Policy.* New York: Macmillan, 1973.

Wert, Jeffry D. *General James Longstreet: The Confederacy's Most Controversial Soldier—A Biography.* New York: Simon & Schuster, 1993.

Woodworth, Steven E. *Davis and Lee at War.* Lawrence: University of Kansas Press, 1995.

Articles

Castel, Albert. "The Historian and the General: Thomas L. Connelly versus Robert E. Lee." *Civil War History* 16 (March 1970): 50–63.

Connelly, Thomas L. "Robert E. Lee and the Western Confederacy: A Criticism of Lee's Strategic Ability." *Civil War History* 15 (June 1969): 116–132.

Naisawald, L. VanLoan. "The Battle of Bristoe Station." *Virginia Cavalcade* 18 (Autumn 1968): 39–47.

Wagstaff, Henry McGilbert, ed. "Letters of Thomas Jackson Strayhorn." *North Carolina Historical Review* 13 (October 1936): 311–334.

Acknowledgments

This book, more than anything else I have ever written, has a particularly strange genesis. I began working with parts of the thesis in the late 1970s when I was a graduate student at Temple University studying under my mentor, Professor Russell F. Weigley. Russ Weigley helped me to shape my interest in the American Civil War, an interest kindled in a youth during the centennial of that struggle, into a framework of critical professionalism. While I subsequently, and quite accidentally, became a naval historian, I never forgot Weigley's injunction that any American military historian "worth his [I am sure in the 1990s he says his or her] salt" had, at one time or another, to write about the War of the Rebellion. Twenty years have passed, but I have finally complied.

I began to collect material for this work and to focus my ideas in the late 1980s, beginning with a draft study of Lee's Bristoe Station campaign. While working in the national capital, I had the opportunity to test out some of my hypotheses on the members of the Civil War Round Tables of Washington, D.C., and Alexandria, Virginia, the membership of which I must thank for their interest and less than hostile reception, considering we were south of the Mason-Dixon line.

After setting the project aside for a few years, I resumed work after I came to East Carolina University in 1991 with the encouragement of Bill Still. When I realized that the work had outgrown the bounds of an article, my friend and agent Fritz Heinzen found a home for the project with John Wiley and Sons. I owe particular thanks to my editor at John Wiley—Hana Umlauf Lane—whose critical comments and questions helped me to focus the study while expanding it. (And if that appears paradoxical, it simply means that you have never had the benefit of working with an editor who knows what she is doing.)

The help and support of a number of individuals and staffs allowed me to complete this project. First, I must thank my excellent and self-motivated research assistants—Darren Poupore and Edwin Combs—who collected archival material for the book as the project expanded. I wish to thank the professional archivists at Duke University's Special Collections and the manuscript department at the Davis Library at the University of North Carolina, Chapel Hill. I offer special thanks to Don Lennon and his staff of the manuscript department at the Joyner Library at East Carolina University. I also wish to thank Patricia Guyette and the Inter-Library Loan staff, also at ECU's Joyner Library.

I must also mention the help of my colleagues and the graduate students in the History Department at ECU, many of whom attended and offered constructive comments on a pair of presentations I gave in 1995 and 1997. I most especially wish to thank our Civil War historian, David E. Long, who read parts of the manuscript and who loaned me stacks of books, and Don Collins, who brought to my attention the Guild Press of Indiana's CD-ROM version of the *Official Records.*

I also wish to thank Dean Keats Sparrow, of ECU's College of Arts and Sciences, for supporting the university's first Civil War Symposium in October 1996. The symposium provided me with a partly unforeseen opportunity to present two pieces of my work to an interested and discerning audience.

I most especially wish to thank the chair of the History Department, Roger Biles, and the members of the Department's Research and Publication Committee during the 1995–1996 academic year for awarding me the Research Semester leave that allowed me to complete this manuscript.

Another special thank-you goes to Brian Andrews of the Geography Department at ECU. After offering to help me with the maps for the book, Brian ended up doing them himself—and making them look better than anything I could have generated.

And, as always, I must thank my ever-patient and supportive wife, Carol, and my children, Ryan and Lisa, who for the past eleven years have lived with a father who has been working under one publishing deadline after another.

Index

troop redeployments and, 91, 93, 103, 127, 129

Lost Dispatch. *See* Special Order 191

Manassas campaigns. *See* First Manassas campaign; Second Manassas campaign

maps of battles, 139–41

Marshall, Charles, 63

Maryland campaign (1862)
    alternatives considered, 6–7
    casualties sustained, 32
    Chantilly battle, 7, 11–12, 139
    commencement of, 8–11
    Confederate missteps, 12–14
    desertion and straggling during, 24–25, 27, 33–34
    events leading to, 1–3, 5–6
    generals' support of, 15–16
    Lee's failed strategy, 32–37, 134
    Lee's letters to Davis, 16–19, 24–25, 26, 36–37
    Lee's plan of action, 20–22, 25–26, 29–30, 63, 65, 67–68, 131, 134
    McClellan's countermoves, 26–29, 34–35, 73
    Potomac crossing, 22–23
    Sharpsburg battle, 30–31, 32, 35, 65, 73, 92
    Special Order 191 and, 26, 28–29, 34, 35, 70, 127

McCabe, James D. Jr., 96

McClellan, George B., 1, 2, 39, 127, 132
    Maryland campaign, 10, 17, 21, 22, 26–28, 31, 34–35, 73, 135

McClendan, William A., 13

McDowell, Irvin, 9, 11, 13

McLaws, Lafayette, 85, 94

Meade, George Gordon, 93, 94, 119, 132
    Bristoe Station campaign and, 95, 96, 98, 99, 100, 102, 103, 105–6, 117, 134
    Gettysburg campaign and, 73, 87, 105, 112

Means, Samuel P., 15

Mexican War, 3–4, 16, 44, 133

Military Academy, U.S. (West Point), 4

Milroy, Robert H., 48, 61, 76

Moltke, Helmuth von, 129

Munford, Thomas T., 14–15

Murfreesboro, battle of (1862–63), 43

Napoléon Bonaparte, 73, 132–33

nationalism, 126

Nelson, Horatio, 66, 67

Nolan, B. P., 15

Ox Hill, battle of. *See* Chantilly, battle of

Pemberton, John Clifford, 53

Pender, William Dorsey, 80, 81

Pendleton, A. S. (Sandy), 81

Peninsula campaign (1862), 2, 5, 32, 69

Pettigrew, James J., 79

Pickett, George, 46, 47, 50, 51

Pickett's Charge (1863), 86–87

Pierce, Franklin, 44

Poague, W. T., 111

Pollock, Abram David, 68

Pope, John, 21
    Maryland campaign, 8–9, 12, 13, 17